AF717684

AN INFINITE JOURNEY

An Infinite Journey

by Jan Lockert

Muse Publications
Fort Yates
1993

Translated from Jan Lockert's *Den uendelige reisen innover*, Hilt & Hansteen, Oslo - publisher
Copyright © Jan Lockert, 1989

English translation from the Norwegian by Pat Shaw
Copyright © Jan Lockert, 1993
All rights reserved. No part of this book may be reproduced, stored in or introduced into a retrieval system, or transmitted in any form or by any means (electronic, mechanical, photocopying, recording or otherwise) without prior written permission of the publisher.

First published in the United States of America, 1993

MUSE PUBLICATIONS
202 Main Street
P.O. Box 511
Fort Yates, ND 58538

Printed in the United States of America

Cover art used with permission of Norwegian publisher

Design and layout by Jean Katus

Text printed on recycled paper

Library of Congress Catalog Card Number 93-77137
ISBN 0-9631750-2-5

To Rosalie

One day, several years ago, I set out on a journey. Not to Costa del Sol or the Far East. But inward, into my inner world. To worlds that have been just as real as those I have encountered by car and boat and plane. It became a journey without a destination. An infinite journey.

This book is about my experiences during this journey of exploration. It is about my everyday life at the same time. The inner world cannot exist without the outer world. And vice versa. Together they make up what we call our total self.

This is a book about a special period of my life, when I woke up to a new insight and perception. When I explored my unconscious and found a hidden universe.

Oslo/Connecticut, February 1989

Jan Lockert

Foreword

What is known, I strip away
I launch all men and women forward with me into the
Unknown...
I know I have the best of time and space, and was never
measured and never will be measured
I tramp a perpetual journey...
Not I, not anyone can travel that road for you,
You must travel it for yourself.

—Walt Whitman

I remember when I first met Jan Lockert, I realized almost immediately that we would become good friends. It was precisely five years ago, November 1987, and we were sitting in a small booth in a restaurant not far from the campus of the Connecticut university where I teach. Jan's companion, the woman he calls Anne in this book, who was also a friend of mine, had brought us together and was remaining uncharacteristically quiet as Jan and I talked, taking the measure of the other.

He was tall, very tan, despite the season, and his face emanated a manly vigor and self-assurance. This man was at ease with himself and though not young, he radiated a youthful vitality and enthusiasm about life that demonstrated unmistakably to me that he had discovered the secret of how to live.

But there was something else that drew me to him even more, and this was the quality that I have never failed to observe in Jan whenever we have been together. When you are with him, you become aware that you are instantly engaged with the *soul* of this man, not merely his persona. There is an immediate sense of *I-Thou* contact, a kind of communion of spirit which leads one very quickly into a depth of conversation and personal rapport that one usually has only with long-time friends. Yet with Jan—and others besides myself have commented on this—you find yourself almost at once on this seemingly already familiar ground of deep intimacy.

So from the start, then, I could see that this man had a secret very much worth knowing, and that in the course of our acquaintanceship, which seemed inevitable, I would learn it. And so began the rich years of our friendship, and of our sometimes mutually intertwined journeys and self-explorations that have led us to spend much time in one another's company on both coasts of the United States, in Jan's native Norway and in the heart of Tuscany where once for three weeks under a pale winter sun we continually sought shelter and interior illumination in its fabled museums and cathedrals and otherwise indulged ourselves in the sensate glories unique to that part of Italy.

None of that, however, will be found in this book. But what is here is far more important: Here, in *An Infinite Journey*, Jan Lockert discloses the secret of that enormous self-possession and extraordinary *élan* that had so impressed me the day we first met in that restaurant. And it turns out, these qualities are not necessarily the innate gifts of Jan's character; they are, instead, largely the results of his own efforts and courageous explorations into the depths of his own soul. Yet the story that is told in this book is not merely Jan's alone—it is also a blueprint for anyone seeking to attain for himself or herself access to one's own authentic self by, as Whitman says, stripping away the known of the ego in order to uncover the vastness of the Cosmos within that is our true being.

An Infinite Journey, then, is a modern narrative illustrating the always timely timeless wisdom of the 42nd fragment of Heraclitus which tells us, "You could not discover the limits of the soul, even if you traveled every road to do so; such is the depth of its meaning." But of course the modern quest for self-knowledge always has its distinct particulars and that is true for this book as well. In Jan Lockert's case, his journey is also and simultaneously the story of his deep, abiding and karmic love for Anne, his spiritual muse and life companion, and his discovery of and increasing involvement with the field of transpersonal psychology and therapy. It was in connection with the latter, beginning in 1982, that Jan came to know and appreciate the value of the methods of self-exploration whose fruits are so evident in this book. These techniques of consciousness-expansion inform much of the applied work of transpersonal psychology and Jan Lockert is an able exponent and exemplar of their benefits. In addition, throughout his book, you will also find frequent reference to the research and insights of some of the leading pioneers of this field, particularly those of Stanislav Grof whose methods of accessing the deep unconscious have won him a worldwide following and an assured niche in the pantheon of depth psychologists whose lineage goes back to Heraclitus himself.

Yet, it is the deeply personal tone of this book, the accounts of Jan's searing and revelatory journeys in the transpersonal realms of the unconscious, and perhaps most of all the compelling and haunting love story with Anne that he tells—the outward mirror to his inner voyages—that will strike you most forcibly and leave the deepest imprint upon you. For this is a book that is likely to stay with you and leave its mark on your psyche long after you have placed it on your bookshelves. In it, you will meet the man I met, you will see the qualities I found in him, and, if you are like me, you will not soon forget him—or the thoughts and desires that his own adventurous self-inquiry may have stimulated in your own soul.

Through his writings and the methods of consciousness-expansion he has used so profitably in his own life, Jan has already helped many persons, particularly in his own country, Norway, in their journeys toward self-knowledge and spiritual fulfillment (he gives only one such example in this book, but it is illustrative of the power of the methods described here). It is my hope that this, his first, book in English will introduce him to a much wider audience and through the methods he espouses will serve to draw many other to what Stanislav Grof has called "the adventure of self-discovery."

As for Jan Lockert himself these days? Well, as you might expect, he has followed his heart into new realms—he has recently published in Norway a well-received novel, *Pi'ilani's Spirit*, he has traveled to exotic locales of the world in search of further experiences for his creative work and he has certainly found that many new persons have come to his door seeking to learn first-hand from him how to gain access to transpersonal states of consciousness. Yet, for all the novelty, there are continuities, too. The inner voyages are still embarked upon, and, yes, his life with his beloved Anne has never ceased though it constantly changes form. Even as

I write these words, Jan is preparing to journey to California once again to be with her for a time. So, as the title of this book promises, the journey continues... and will continue, for Jan Lockert's version of "Song of Myself" is of course the universal story of our unending quest to realize what it is to be truly alive in a world of unfathomable mystery.

Kenneth Ring, Ph.D.
November 1992

PART ONE

ANNE

We shall not cease from exploration
And the end of all our exploring
Will be to arrive where we started
And know the place for the first time.

T.S. Eliot

The only journey of exploration
of value is the journey to
one's inner self.

C.G. Jung

I am lying on the couch in the living room. Here in our home in Connecticut. It is five o'clock in the morning. Anne is asleep upstairs. I have just been awakened by a dream.

I dreamed I was in a room in a cellar. The only way out was through a narrow shaft. It led upward. It was as if some kind of conveyor belt were moving in the shaft. Once inside, one was carried forward whether one wanted to be or not. I knew I had to get out. But further up the shaft narrowed. It became so tight that there was hardly any opening. Impossible to get my head and shoulders through. I would be stuck. Squeezed to death. I couldn't possibly get out in there. I had awakened and been afraid. In a waking state I realized that I had to go through that shaft. Out. Now or never. I had to get out!

I had stolen out of bed without waking Anne. And now I am lying here, on the couch, one Sunday morning. But it had started Friday evening...

During the past seven years I have been engaged in modern consciousness research, studying in The United States and Australia. After considerable training, I have taught myself a technique of leaving the consciousness of everyday life and entering other realms of my consciousness. These other realms exist. Worlds that are totally different from the one we experience around us, and just as real. In order to experience them, we must be able to let ourselves go and abandon the control. On Friday evening I had set out on such an inner journey. I had left the everyday consciousness, and entered a totally different state of consciousness. Not a dream, but a layer of the unconscious to which we do not have daily access. This may sound incomprehensible to the reader, but I must ask you to let *yourself* go—read on—.

Then, perhaps, something will be revealed. Friday evening I had made the necessary preparations, and the journey was in progress. When I was well out of my ordinary consciousness, a mysterious being appeared. Not literally, but from within. It was a figure of a woman. She gave me considerable trouble. I resisted something that she wanted my body to do. That is to say, my body resisted. It made a lot of movements that I had not asked it to make, nor had any part in. It was then that I realized that it had been "programmed." It was not being controlled by my present consciousness alone. It had clearly been "programmed" or "designed" for something, I don't know when or by whom. It contained an energy that was incomprehensible to me. It was as if someone had been directing it. Behind what *my* brain had initiated. At any rate, it had been told to do something that it was unwilling to do. I had a suspicion that it was to be born.

Patience, I thought. Patience. The root of all evil is *im*patience.

I had been lying there with my stiff neck. The Being said:

"Don't you want to?" She looked at me with a smile. "That neck of yours has been saying 'No' to life. In all likelihood, you said 'No' to being born, the last time you entered the world. It's as if you've been saying 'No' to being here on earth."

This was quite a jolt. But the words hit home. She was right.

She said, "Saying 'No' to life is saying 'No' to God, the Divine Reality, The Ultimate Reality, or whatever you prefer to call it. That is one attitude. Another would be to say 'Yes,' and surrender."

I said, "Surrendering is not my cup of tea. Willpower is most important to me."

It may be that I have defied the Will of God. But, to me, the Will of God was represented by intolerant people in the place where I grew up. They made capital of it. I couldn't accept that. My willpower has enabled me to survive so well. I thought: It may not be so well after all, but...

The Female Being smiled even more broadly. "Your willpower is your limitation. Perhaps now is the time to assume a different attitude. Your will is no longer necessary. You may be attuned to higher forces and adapt yourself accordingly."

She left after this philosophical discussion, and I lay there exhausted.

° ° °

And now I am lying here on this Sunday morning, after the frightening dream. It is still dark. It is a long couch. It consists of several sections. I have a pillow under my neck. If I take away the pillow, I will be lying quite flat.

I know that in order to get on with my life, I have to go through the shaft of the dream whether I am squeezed to death or not. There is no other way. I have to have the courage to go through it. This is why I have set out on a new inner journey, into my unconscious. I have a guilty conscience because I am doing this without letting her know up there—my dear wife Anne. But I don't want to upset her. She is not feeling well at present. Going through a dark night of the soul. Doesn't know why. She is so self-sacrificing, and wants so much to help others. But she neglects helping herself.

Now I am lying here, experiencing her. It is as if I am entering her, going under her skin. I *am* her. She is so complacent, wants to please me so much. But where is *she*? Where is *her* person in this world? Suddenly I understand how much stronger I am than she is. Suddenly I "see" it: Her life consists of getting away from me.

I think: Strange formulation...her life consists of... Inside myself, I say to her: "My dear, I understand that what you are struggling with, what you are afraid of facing and what may be making you so depressed, is the fact that you must tear yourself away from me."

I can see it clearly, I am too strong, I am crushing her, everything that is her, I am stifling her. She is unable to breathe. How difficult it must be for her to include me in her life! She is acting out of loyalty and duty.

My God, what a discovery! Will I have to lose her? I must tell her this. It may help her, bring the knots out into the open. Even if she may think that I want to get rid of her. When the opposite is the case. But I must tell her what I have seen. And I "see" more. Behind me I see another shadow, the one she *really* has to get away from: her domineering father. Not only the old father who lives fifteen minutes away from us, perhaps. But the father inside her. Now it is easier for me to understand the formulation: Her life consists of...

My journey continues. Now it is "me" who comes to me. I encounter "myself," and I make a new discovery: I am constantly trying to talk myself out of being *myself*.

Something strange happens. I am myself, but, at the same time, I am observing myself. It is as if I am going outside my brain. Observing the way it functions. I see how much of its energy it uses to gloss over things. Fabricating explanations which are supposed to make me look good. Now it is trying to find an excuse for Anne about why I am lying here by myself. Lord, how it wants to embellish a story. This must have become automatic. It must go on all day long without my noticing it. What a mess! This has to stop!

My body has started moving again. Curling up and stretching out. I think: The programming! The staging. It curls up and stretches out. It aches! My neck, and all the way down along my back. I stretch and stretch. The pillow is gone. I am lying flat. There is a tremendous force that is playing havoc with my body. I stretch until every joint creaks. Stretch until I am several inches longer, at least several inches. Stretch myself through the fear that awakened me from the dream. Then I curl up. "I" am not the one who is controlling this. It is as if there is a director behind it. I feel like throwing up. I think: Now I'm dying! I can't stand it any longer!

It is pulling and tearing at my body. Squeezing it. The pain is terrible. I curl up, try to avoid it. But it intensifies. Something is about to happen. And something is holding back. Suddenly the Female Being is there. What a radiance! There is a light around her.

She says, "Surely you must understand that you cannot be born before you let go of your old ego."

Yes. I understand. I, myself, am blocking the way. The man who entered this world, the one with the authority, he is the one who is standing in the way. Let him go! Get rid of him! But it isn't easy. I realize that it is a question of a total transformation of personality.

This has been going on for several hours. I am exhausted. My stomach is in knots. My neck aches. My body feels as if it is being squeezed together. Regularly. More and more often. Suddenly I discover that I am pressing the thumb and middle finger of my right hand against my temples—like a claw, I think, yes, like a pair of forceps. Now, where did that come from? "I" wasn't the one who had placed my hand there.

The pain increases. Goes beyond all bounds. In a flash I am in a cave filled with blood. The exit is blocked by boulders. Then it happens: The shaft, the shaft gives way! I am not being squeezed to death. What had previously been boulders, is now flesh, warm, living flesh. I see the veins. It yields as long as I yield, I can just relax, soft and warm, it engulfs me, the forceps pressing against my temples, my breathing stops, body tensing, and *then*: Release! Oh Lord, release! I am through! Oh my God, I am through!

I sink back. My body relaxes. My shoulders settle into place. My neck straightens out. I am through. It is done! Good God, it is done. Mucus loosens from my throat and fills my mouth. It comes of itself. I swallow it. My throat is cleared. I belch. Belch as I have never belched before.

Then peace. I am lying on my back. Filled with gratitude. I think: I have been born. Being born is a matter between my God and myself. First impulse: Jubilation. I have been born rejoicing. I am grateful to Anne, up there. In a strange way I feel that she has helped me. I whisper: "You are my mother. You have given birth to me." It rushes through my mind: The title of a play, perhaps: "All My Mothers."

Silence. Complete silence. Born. To what? A creative life, I think. A lonely life? Perhaps. The Luminous Being is standing there. She says, "Tell! Look around you and tell!"

So *this* is the message, the task: Tell!

Then comes doubt. Do I believe this? Do I *believe* this? Or is this merely an illusion?

The Luminous Being says, "You *must believe*!"

I have been reborn into this world. The question occurs to me: Do I want this? Do I want to be in this world? To assume my duties. To take responsibility for my life. The pain in my neck comes back. My head drops forward. I feel the old sensation of hopelessness. My brain begins to churn, to find ways of escape.

The Luminous Being says, "Accept! Accept your brain, all of your thoughts. Let them come. Accept! Everything is good."

Yes, it is good. I calm down again. This is what I want. I accept the challenge. "Thy will be done! Not mine."

I lie quietly, allow my thoughts to wander. Look at them. Observe them. One thought gets stuck: Must I really be parted from my beloved upstairs? I dismiss the thought from my mind. Repress it. And I observe the way it immediately settles in my body. A stomach muscle is knotted. A muscle in my throat stiffens. I follow the nerve fibers in my body. Aha! So this is the way the psychosomatic ailment originates! How interesting. I take the thought out again. Hold onto it. Face up to it. I feel the way my stomach muscle lets go, and the muscle in my throat. It is incredible. I have access to the "mechanism" in myself.

Take whatever comes. Don't let it enter your body! Be honest now!

Where does it come from, this automatic reflex of embellishing, of being unwilling to face things, of repressing? I close my eyes, follow my breathing, go inward. My mother comes to me. But not my mother the way I remember her—old and grey. I see a young woman. Smiling, beautiful. So incredibly young. And so dazzlingly beautiful. I had forgotten this woman. Oh, how I must have loved her! I must have been afraid of losing her love. Or, rather, wanted to win it. My first, unrequited love. Embellish, rather than be rejected by her.

Something strange happens. I am a fetus. A fetus inside her. And suddenly I have a feeling of guilt because of her big stomach. I am the one who has spoiled her beautiful body...

Three hours have passed. It is daylight. I hear Anne get out of bed and go into the bathroom. The time has come to share my experience. So far, it had to be a lonely road.

I go upstairs. Anne comes toward me. I put my arms around her. Hold her tight.

"I've been born," I whisper jubilantly.

"Tell me about it!" she says.

And I tell her. I say, "My life has acquired meaning. *I* have acquired meaning."

"You have acquired faith," she says. "Tell me what you believe in."

"I believe in my own process," I reply. "Believing in one's own process is what it's all about... I believe that I am on my way. That what happens is right. That there is a Divine Guidance. And that everything that happens has meaning. Even though we do not understand it."

"Good for you!" she exclaims warmly.

I think: Later, later I will tell her what I have experienced as her. What I discovered. It won't be easy.

The morning sun has entered our bedroom. A bird, completely red, is sitting on the branch outside.

"Look!" we both say at the same time.

° ° °

How much progress has the world made? In the year 1600 A.D., Giordano Bruno was burned at the stake because he claimed that there were many worlds, and that the Earth could not be the center of the Universe. How frightening is it, even today, for one to open the door to one's inner self, and visit the worlds that are there?

Man has carried on research, and knows a great deal about chemistry, physics and astronomy. But how much do we know about the consciousness? The human mind? Practically nothing. If we believe that the highest knowledge is to know "thyself," then why is it so provocative to enter the mind?

I do as I have been told: Tell. This is going to be a controversial story.

The man who comes back through the
Door in the Wall will never be quite
the same as the man who went out.
He will be wiser but less cocksure,
happier but less self-satisfied,
humbler in acknowledging his ignorance
yet better equipped to understand the
relationship of words to things, of
systematic reasoning to the unfathomable
Mystery which it tries, forever vainly,
to comprehend.

Aldous Huxley

I continue on my way. I have a long journey ahead of me. A number of journeys. I quite like to be on my way. There have been times when I thought that being on my way was the only thing worth living for. To greater insight. Knowledge. Understanding. At other times it was love. Perhaps they belong together.

I was also on my way, in a literal sense, one day in September 1982. I was sitting in a tiny local plane on my way from Los Angeles to Monterey. The plane landed at every airstrip. It went down every ten minutes. The hot air quivered over the California sands. The plane vibrated. Night had finally fallen.

The day is long during the eleven-hour stretch from Copenhagen to Los Angeles—a nine-hour difference of time in the same direction as the sun. The sunset over the Pacific was orange. A gigantic sun was swallowed up by the ocean. One moment it was a disc that could roll along the horizon. But no one was pushing it. And then it went down.

I was on my way to the Esalen Institute at Big Sur. I was going to take part in a four-week seminar with Dr. Stanislav Grof. It had the enticing title, "The Mystical Quest."

It was dark when we landed in Monterey. There was a surprise waiting for me at the airport. Kathleen, Grof's secretary, had come to meet me. Why me, of all the 34 participants? I had been prepared to spend the night at a hotel, and continue the next day. She said that she had liked my letters, my style of writing, so she wanted to come and pick me up herself. There couldn't have been a nicer start to my studies.

Big Sur is an hour away by car, along the coastal road south of Monterey, the most beautiful drive in the U.S.A. The road winds along the steep, colorful cliffs at the edge of the Pacific. As we stepped out of the car in the garden of the Institute, there was the fragrance of the sea and thousands of plants in the hot night air. I had arrived at Esalen, one of the leading avant-garde institutes in America, where physics and mysticism meet, body and soul, the philosophies and religions of East and West. Both despair and wanderlust had started me on this journey. Despair, because I felt that I had come to a point in life where I was caught in a trap. Wanderlust, because I have always enjoyed being...well...on my way.

I always wanted to be a writer. I started on a small scale when I was fifteen. But my faith in myself was not much. After reading Knut Hamsun's novel *Pan* until the pages were in tatters, it wasn't surprising that my short stories were a hopeless regurgitation of Lt. Glahn's reminiscences. Then I turned to Ibsen. The idea of creating people who talked to each other fascinated me. For a long time I had surrounded myself with imaginary friends with whom I conversed. If there were no real people who understood what I was talking about, there was nothing better than to invent a few characters and carry on a profound conversation this way.

I chose a practical profession. I studied for my Master's degree at the Copenhagen School of Economics and Business Administration. Five or six years later I bitterly regretted it, and started writing plays. My first play was called "The Judge." The action took place in the past, the present and the future—in several alternative futures. The head of the Oslo New Theater stared at me for half an hour in his office, probably wondering what sort of young man this was, who could cook up something like that. Later, things improved. "The Man Who Climbed the Ladder" was accepted by the

National Theater both in Oslo, and in Bergen. But it was eventually performed at a less prestigious theater.

Consequently, my faith in myself as a writer was still modest. I gradually became absorbed in professional management. I started my own consulting firm. I was probably born with a talent for management. As a child I had a rabbit farm, more than 50 rabbits. I had the children in my street help build the cages. I appointed them all bosses, one for the hammering, one for the sawing, etc., and they all worked to their heart's content.

Anyway, in the 1970's I found myself on the board of directors of 12-15 companies, half of which I chaired. What was supposed to be a normal working day divided between management and writing—"rendering unto Cæsar that which was Cæsar's, and to God that which was God's"—became a 60-hour week in the palace of Cæsar.

But even though I was regarded as a pillar of society in many circles, I realized that I had to escape in order to continue my own personal quest. One day I had had enough. I packed four suitcases, put them in the back of my car and left, without destination, heading south.

I was gone for six months. I rented a couple of rooms in a tiny village in the South of France. There I cautiously began a few tentative exercises in composition. I wrote a light comedy called "A Piece of Love." It was about a good friend—a charming and knowledgeable lady who also sold her charms. I sent it to the National Theatre in Oslo. The trouble with the play was that it was based too much on reality. After a long time, I received a few lines. I was quite surprised when I read: "The author can write dialogue, but he should steer clear of material that is so far-fetched and has little to do with reality." Well, that's the way it goes. One must tell lies in order to be believed.

When I came back from France, I knew that I had to turn another leaf in the Book of Life. I had read the old page once too often. In the course of these business years, I had tried to keep up with what was being written in other fields—especially psychology. I read Sigmund Freud, Aldous Huxley, Erich Fromm, Pierre Teilhard de Chardin, P.D. Ouspensky, James Hillman and others. For several years I had been concentrating on Carl Gustav Jung, whose mystical bent had attracted me considerably. With varying degrees of diligence, I had started practicing Yoga. And I meditated. It began to dawn on me that, in reality, I was shut out from my inner self, and that perhaps only the ambitionless and self-denying meditation of the East could open the door to the unknown. Only by letting go, without goals, without desires and willpower, could the unknown be revealed. If I insisted on drawing the landscape myself, it would still be quite grey. I remember thinking: Perhaps it is true that when we think, we are not thinking, but when we are not thinking, then we are thinking.

A friend called my attention to Stanislav Grof, psychiatrist and one of the leading authorities on consciousness research. A Czech, who had been residing in the U.S. for the past several decades. I got hold of his books and started to read. It gradually became clear to me that Grof's thirty years of researching the human mind, and the results he had achieved were epoch-making. If I could work with him, undreamed-of possibilities would open up. I could no longer stand business life, I was feeling quite frustrated as a writer. Not to mention as a human being. I retained the mask. A long life had taught me to retain the mask. Now it would soon be apparent that I had to learn how to throw it off. I had to make a complete break with my former life. I wrote to Stanislav Grof and explained why I wanted to come.

It was a happy day when I held his answer in my hand: I was welcome!

And one morning we were sitting there, some thirty people on pillows, on the floor in the great room of The Big House. For four weeks we were going to be a family. Most of them were psychologists from many lands; several doctors, a lawyer from Zurich, a film producer from Vienna, the director of a drama school in Germany—and myself. We were evenly divided between the sexes. Common to us all was the search for deeper insight and understanding, the urge to explore oneself in order to be more capable of helping others. I had been lodged in "The Star Room" with Paul, an Australian physicist, who had just settled in the U.S. The Star Room was an annex of the old, main building. Outside the window, enormous silvery tree trunks reached up to the sky. And less than a stone's throw away was the ocean.

The sunlight filtered in to us through the leaves. Stan Grof had come into "The Big Room." A husky man, more than six feet tall, with a striking charisma. There was an inner sparkle in his brown eyes. He started to speak—simple, quiet, soothing words. Trust, was the thought that entered my mind. I could trust this man. Have confidence in him. I had traveled a long way from the boardrooms of Oslo.

Intellectually, these four weeks would provide us with considerable knowledge, with excellent lecturers: from mythology to nuclear physics, from psychology to the religions of the East and West. But most important of all, perhaps, were the inner journeys we were going to take. Two or three times a week, we ourselves were going to "travel." And the same number of times we would learn how to be guides, and assist someone else who was "traveling."

Since then I have gone on a number of inner journeys. That is to say, I have left my everyday consciousness and entered other layers of my consciousness—or should I say my unconscious. The same place where people go who have near-death experiences. In this unusual state of consciousness, I have relived episodes from my life, all the way back to infancy. Relived them as if I *were* the child. This therapy brought me even deeper. I relived my birth. A child may experience being born as dying—being squeezed to death—when the mother is bearing down and there is still no way out. And I went beyond my personal life, beyond time and space, into what is called "transpersonal experiences" (i.e., transpersonal = exceeding, overstepping the personal). This was a combination of therapy and training.

Now, during the journey that had begun on this dramatic Sunday morning, I have the feeling that I have embarked on a journey of discovery of a different dimension. That it does not concern me alone, but that there is a collective message in what I am being asked to do. I feel that this time there is a greater spiritual dimension. That it is more research than therapy, and that I am supposed to write about it. Everything I have experienced has been a necessary preparation.

The technique developed by Grof, which I learned at Esalen and with which I have continued to work, is called "Holotropic Therapy." It is a therapy that is free of medication, a combination of a special breathing technique called "hyperventilation" (based on Yoga traditions that are thousands of years old), evocative music, as well as working with the tensions of the body.

The breathing technique makes it possible to "turn off the brain," and penetrate into deep layers of the unconscious. Gradually, as the session progresses, the latent tensions in the body are intensified to such an extent that the underlying causes are forced to the surface. This makes it possible to focus on them and break them down. One relives important traumatic experiences from one's life and, to an even greater extent, of birth—the most dramatic event in a person's life. Gradually, transpersonal experiences also crop up.

The fundamental principle of holotropic therapy is that one relies on the self-healing ability of the mind and the body's own intrinsic wisdom, which can be mobilized once they are summoned. If one is able to let go of one's control and surrender oneself to the deeper layers of the unconscious, the final result of the sessions of hyperventilation will be a new and beneficial psychic balance and lasting satisfaction.

In addition, Grof believes that the symptoms in themselves are indications of healing. A therapist is not someone who *does* something, but someone who assists the process of healing that is taking place in the client. Neither the therapist nor the client has to *understand*, one must *rely on* the fact that what is taking place is supposed to take place in order to heal. The healing has little to do with what the therapist believes or understands.

However, it is entirely necessary to have a competent assistant, someone who can help you through critical situations. You cannot let go of your control, while, at the same time, being responsible for a safe and undisturbed course of action.

Holotropic or experiential therapy produces more basic results than conventional therapy because it is concerned with the deepseated roots of our mental state, that cannot be traced to childhood experiences alone. Under these lie the influences from our birth and transpersonal material. And while conventional therapy may take years without far-reaching results, experiential therapy may cause dramatic changes in personality in the course of a limited number of sessions.*

According to Grof, who has conducted several thousand holotropic sessions: "These techniques can open access to areas of experience for which our culture does not have an adequate conceptual framework. In spite of the fact that such experiences as perinatal sequences and transpersonal phenomena can be very healing and transformative, an uninformed Westerner tends to fight against them and block them because they appear strange, bizarre, or even indicative of severe psychopathology."

I will render several perinatal and transpersonal experiences below.

Grof says: "Holotropic therapy favors activation of the unconscious, which is so powerful that it results in a non-ordinary state of consciousness." The main contribution of this therapy is the recognition of the healing, transformative and evolutionary potential of reliving unconscious material through these states. Grof calls it "the experiential journey of the soul into the voluntary prison of matter, and its liberation from this prison, finding its way back to itself."

At Esalen, the sessions took place in "The Big Room." Half of the participants lay on the floor, breathing, while each of the others took care of his/her individual "traveler," helping them remove the armor of their muscles. The fact that there were so many people in the room did not disturb the individual. In the non-ordinary state of consciousness, the "traveler" had little contact with the outside world. On

---

*Readers who would like to study holotropic methods more closely are referred to Stanislav Grof's book: *The Adventure of Self-Exploration*, 1987.

the contrary, the "energy" that flowed from so many people in the same room was tremendously stimulating.

Watching over a person who is undertaking such a journey is a deeply moving and rewarding experience in itself. A feeling of caring and participation, which gives a veneration for life and the labyrinths of the mind.

It usually takes twenty minutes, with deep and rapid breathing, for me to transcend, go out of my daily consciousness and into other realms. Thereafter, the journey may continue for one or two hours or even longer. It is easier, the more sessions one has had. Crucial is to have the courage to let go of control. To be honest. To trust that there are higher forces within you—or coming to you—to which you may safely surrender "yourself."

In his book, *The Doors of Perception*, Aldous Huxley described the brain as a "censoring valve." It is a reduction in the efficiency of this valve which takes place when you let go of the control and open yourself to other states of consciousness. A change occurs in the chemical processes of the brain, which causes different aspects of the human unconscious to become conscious. "This permits entry into consciousness of experiences, visionary or mystical, from 'out there,'" he wrote. Where you are now in your own development, and the circumstances under which the sessions take place, are decisive for the type of experiences you have. This is not only true of the settings, but also of the preparation, insight and understanding with which you go to the session. I myself fast for a day or two and meditate for several hours before a session.

° ° °

Last night I was again awakened by a dream. I dreamed I was in a large house. It was my house. There were people everywhere. I knew many of them. Most of the people who have meant something to me during my life. I was standing on the first floor. There was a succession of rooms, one after the other, large rooms where people were going in and out. A broad stairway led up to the second floor. I went up. There were more rooms up there, great halls. Several people, perhaps not as many as on the first floor. Some were standing, some were sitting on the steps. A new flight of stairs led to the third floor. I had never been there before. Several rooms. But only a few people. I saw that there was a fourth floor. Perhaps it continued. Indefinitely? I didn't know that my house contained so many floors and rooms.

° ° °

It is true that the mind contains many rooms. I have been thinking about this dream all day. Decided that, this evening, I would crack the door open to some of them.

I am lying on the bed in our bedroom. Ready for a new inner journey. Anne is dozing beside me. I will wake her in a little while. Dear, drowsy Anne. I am tingling with excitement and expectation.

It is still light outside. We have a large bedroom. The wall opposite the bed consists only of windows. I look out onto the crowns of big old trees. It is autumn. The leaves are glowing with color, endless nuances of red. Through the foliage I see the river—broad, calm, one can barely see the water flowing past.

I am lying there, waiting for the journey to begin. As I said, it's a question of letting go, abandoning oneself, "getting out of the head," I call it. Not until we let go of control do we realize how strongly we are controlling. We cling to control. This is where our limitations lie. This need to control all the time comes from fear, of course—the fear of what will happen if we don't. What would emerge? But I also wonder if there isn't an element of "avarice" in this. The fact that we don't want to miss something. And so we cling to dry cerebral activity—because we believe that this is what will give us new knowledge. Don't realize that it is when we "turn it off" that we open up to a deeper insight and intuition.

It is the bane of humankind that we have to use rational intellect in order to find an answer to every question. Adam did eat of the Tree of Knowledge. Was this an episode? An accident? Or was it a link in the process, the human process on this planet, the process of the unconscious, that which may be our immortal soul? The whole answer to what humankind is depends, in fact, on the answer to this.

Is it a coincidence that we human beings should acquire such an insight into Nature that we are able to copy it when it comes to nuclear energy? Or is it the intention of The Creator that some day we shall come up to His/Her shoulders? Stephen W. Hawking, the English physicist, believes that we will come close to an answer to why we and the universe exist, the day we discover the unifying law of physics. I wonder if the final answers are to be found in another dimension. A dimension of consciousness.

The journey begins. I feel the first quivers. My entire body is trembling and shaking. I am not afraid. It appears as if this is the passage that I must go through, the transit, in order to enter other realms. I do not know if these are tensions in the body that are being discharged. Or energies that are awakening in me. This is called "Kundalini Energy." I only know that I must yield to what is taking place.

The trembling lasts about fifteen minutes. Then comes a vast openness, an awareness of the body. I "see" that, when the body builds up a resistance to following the mind, and vice versa, this may cause illness. I again "see" how something in my body must have been staged a long, long time ago. From childhood, from birth, even further back, before conception perhaps. And I "see" that illness may be transferred by the genes. It is as if I can see that the body has *its* consciousness, independent of other consciousness. That the body has its own memory of pain, for example. It strikes me that when one has received anaesthesia during an operation, the body will still "remember" the pain which "the other consciousness" was spared.

The next thing I experience is that I am in an aquarium. I am surrounded by thick walls of Plexiglas. Anne is standing outside with two of my children and several friends. I am unable to hear them. They are unable to hear me. I cannot reach them.

I have a terrible need to be free. It is exerting pressure. I think: I am losing my mind! Then the Luminous Being is standing there. She smiles, says: "Lose... your mind!" I feel how strongly I am controlling. And I know that if I can let go, there is a chance that I can get hold of that which is *not* controlled by the intellect.

I think: What is freedom? What do I want freedom for? I *have* freedom. I have the freedom to do whatever I like. External freedom. But the point is *inner* freedom. I "see" that my body is not the only thing that has been staged. My thoughts have also been programmed. I look at my thoughts as they appear. How many free, spontaneous thoughts? How many compulsive thoughts? How many thoughts that have been thought by others? How many thoughts that go in circles?

I follow the thoughts. It is disturbing to see how they are fenced in. I have been indoctrinated, pure and simple. When? And by whom? The thoughts are guided by something "behind," I don't know what it is. Freedom of *thought* is what I want. Many thoughts aim at "pretending," and then I am not free. If I look around for recognition, am dependent on what "they" think, then I am not free. I "see" that I must have the courage to exist without confirmation. Rely entirely on myself. Only then can the spontaneous "newborn" thought, my own thought—if I may call it that—have a chance.

The journey continues. I experience a boundless need for contact. Cautiously, I touch Anne. She is lying beside me, looking at me. I gaze into her eyes. Through them. I see that she is a mystery. She is a mystery to me. She is a mystery to herself. What is a mystery? A mystery is something we shall never find the answer to. Otherwise, it would be no mystery.

"Darling," I whisper. I think she is experiencing what is going on inside me. I think: Contact is a willingness to share one's inner life. Not only by *saying* something, but also by opening up to layers deep in oneself. Sharing—beyond words—simply by opening up. Sharing that which cannot be expressed in words. It is in these layers that love has its roots.

We look into each others' eyes. We caress each other with our eyes. Life awakens. First at the bottom of the spine. Then it rises Along the back, spreads to the shoulders, neck, arms, legs, the entire body. God! To be filled with life! I give Anne of my life through my eyes. I do not touch her. The energy flows between us without touching. We laugh with each other. Is the Luminous Being standing in the corner, smiling? It wouldn't surprise me.

I make love to Anne. She has dyed her hair blonde, and has brown eyes. Now I think the features of her face are changing. She becomes darker. She looks Indian. I am making love to an Indian woman. When, during which period of time, did I have an Indian woman?

Her face is constantly changing. I look at this face. My Anne. Now I see in her eyes—in the finely chiseled nose—my bride, my very young bride from centuries past. Beautiful. Beautiful. I hold her face between my hands and read it. What joy, what delight to have such a beautiful young bride! And I read more. Now I see a little girl. About seven years old, eyes aglow with curiosity. Mischievous, naughty. An appetite for life. And I read the slumbering woman, the fourteen-year old, the dreams, the first yearning. I see a few tears. Her face has grown softer. A touch of melancholy at the mouth. Something has happened to her, something that has marked her. I think I can see what it is. Her eyes look inward and far beyond.

Slowly, cautiously, we make love. In her eyes I read tenderness. It is more than sexual. More than erotic. Anne is an angel. An angel who has come in a bodily form in order to help transcend that form. I close my eyes. I see beautiful landscapes. Golden landscapes. I don't think they are on earth. I don't know if they are from other ages, whether they exist or whether I am creating them. The green rolling meadows, the red mountains, the slender trees as high as the sky. Never have I felt so creative, had such visions. And I understand, I understand that erotic energy is creative energy, the Source itself, the primeval force, that the road to creativity, to imagination, even to the spiritual world, goes through this divine energy.

Afterwards, we lie quietly on our backs with our eyes closed, holding hands.

Then it happens: I am standing before The Great Door. A big, majestic, double door. It opens and I look inside, into the Promised Land. I want to go in through that door. But I know that it is Death's door. To go in through that door means to die. I hesitate. The door is wide open, but I am unable to enter. I am not exactly afraid. But life is holding me back. The life that I have not finished with. I take a firmer grip on Anne's hand.

The door closes. I want to go inside. There is nothing I would rather do. But it is too late. The door does not open again. I become desperate. It is as if I am not found worthy. Am I asking too much? Am I asking too much, too soon? I have a long way to go.

° ° °

It has grown dark. I am lying on my back, breathing deeply, quickly and regularly. I feel that secret forces are taking complete control of me. I am being carried away.

My back is beginning to ache, up toward my neck. What is happening to me? I have never felt such pain. I curl up in bed. Gasp for breath. Anne looks at me with fright. I am unable to speak. I cannot explain. I am being drawn into a maelstrom of pain. Beyond everything.

° ° °

Anne says that two hours have passed. I am surprised that I am in the bedroom. I have been in so many other places. Common to them all was the pain, the suffering. And I always felt it in my shoulders and neck. I try to remember, and tell her.

I was in prison. In a concentration camp. I experienced it as Hell. Dead, putrefying people lay all around me. A degradation beyond comparison. Someone had been beating me over my neck and shoulders. I was unable to stand. I crouched down on the ground, clawing the dirt with my hands. My breathing stopped. My head was filled with silence.

It was at the first light of dawn. Hundreds of years ago. I had been hanged. The pain in my neck was excruciating. I was hanging on a wall, on stones covered with green slime. Two others were hanging on my right. In front of me I could see the castle, with windows and turrets. Steps led down to the left. There was a landing where we were hanging. Then the steps continued up along the wall to the right. Behind the castle was a valley that ended in a forest. The pain in my neck exploded, my head fell forward as I drew my last breath.

I was on a battlefield. I was fighting. I was dressed in a red, white and blue uniform. I fell backward. An enemy soldier stood over me with his lance upraised. He thrust the lance through my heart.

I was standing on a steep stairway, on the next to the top step. A chieftain stood at the top. He was my brother. He stood with his sword lifted above me. My own sword was heavy in my hand. I cried: "Why should I stand here like a loser? Why can't I be your equal?" I turned and left. Since then, I wandered about, to foreign shores. For hundreds of years. I had ships. And I went ashore. But I was homeless. Rootless. I had been defeated because I *felt* defeated. I was every man who has been defeated.

I was an old man. I dragged myself through the snow. Thinly dressed. Freezing. Exhausted from hunger. The drifting snow stung my face.

Anne looks at me silently while I talk. What happened? Why should I experience all this suffering? It occurs to me: Was this the beginning of a process of purification? In order that some day I would be able to go through the Great Door? I had understood that I was unworthy. And Heaven knows, I needed purifying. Perhaps it isn't such a bad idea after all, this much maligned symbol of "Purgatory." According to *The Tibetan Book of the Dead*, man really has enough to contend with during the first period after death.

These were not *my* sufferings. I have never experienced any of this. Not in this life, at any rate. My shoulders and neck suffered most. Where did these experiences come from? Were they from previous lives?

Stanislav Grof believes that in the deepest layers of our unconscious, we have access to all consciousness. Everything that has been created on this planet, indeed, in the whole universe. That consciousness is like the sub-atomic web in the world of matter. Every single part contains the whole. (I discuss this in greater detail in the second half of the book.)

Carl Gustav Jung formulated the theory of the "collective unconscious," which links all people together in a common spiritual heritage. Was this what I had experienced?

Have I had access to, and experienced the sufferings of "everyone," the suffering of humanity, the hard lot of humankind on this earth? I believe that being human on this earth means to suffer, being able to *acknowledge* that we are part of suffering. Perhaps this is a kind of collective responsibility of humankind. I think we must face this destiny of man, be conscious of it, and not suppress it. Maybe the feeling that one is participating in the life of humankind is as much a key to mental health, as assuming responsibility for one's own life. If this is done superficially, I am afraid that a vital dimension will be lost. A dimension of compassion, at any rate. But we must not get bogged down in the suffering. I think we must take it with us. Integrate it into our personality, but not let it dominate us.

I do not really regard myself as a Christian. And Jesus, as the son of God, has never been a reality for me. But now I have a better understanding of what is meant by bearing the suffering of all people. A wave of love for Jesus surges through me, I suddenly feel a relationship with this man.

° ° °

I have gotten something to think about. Up to now I have thought that *I* could stand at the wheel, map and steer a course that I, myself, have drawn. Now I have been flung out into the whirlpool without understanding the forces I am dealing with or where they are taking me.

My neck and back feel sore but relaxed. It is as if I have gotten rid of a yearlong burden. Yearlong? Centurylong? Who knows?

True reality is immeasurable and boundless, and true insight sees the immeasurable and the boundless as the essence of existence.

Stanislav Grof

The stay at Esalen changed my life. It opened my eyes to how limited it had been. During my stay I met Alfred Foote, an Australian clergyman and psychologist who became my good friend. Alf was in charge of a hospital in Melbourne which had as its goals helping people who were dependent on alcohol and narcotics. He used Grof's holotropic therapy on the clients. This interested me so much that I went to Australia the following year, stayed with my friend for a month and accompanied him daily in his work at the hospital.

Alf concentrated primarily on the traumas of birth, which he felt were a fundamental cause of the dependence. He believed that dependence on alcohol originates in Basic Perinatal Matrix II, in the phase Grof calls "No Exit"—where the birth is in progress, the mother is exerting pressure, but there is still no opening. Those, in particular, who have been stuck during this experience, will feel cooped up, hopeless, that there is no end to the misery.

Alf believed that dependence on narcotics originates more from the phase called "the titanic struggle" (BPM III), the struggle to move ahead in the birth canal, the craving for delivery, ecstasy, enlightenment. When—during a series of sessions—the patient, more or less directly or symbolically, has re-experienced the pain, the fear and the aggression that must have remained after these experiences of birth, he/she is released from the unconscious burden which they have caused.

The results were amazing. After fifteen years of activity, Alf was able to show that 75% of his patients developed a normal relationship to alcohol. Among those who were dependent on narcotics, the percentage was somewhat lower.

Jung believed that behind the craving for chemical stimuli, like alcohol and narcotics, is a search for a spiritual, transcendental experience (transcendental—exceeding the limits of ordinary experience). Jung thought that only a deeper experience of this kind could counteract the craving for these stimuli. To him, the most important incentive in the human psyche was not biological, as it was to Freud, but spiritual. "Spiritual" is not the same as "religious." It may be defined as a contact with higher forces or God—the way the individual conceives of the Divinity. Jung's fundamental assumption was that the spiritual element is an organic and integrated part of the psyche. Grof has written: "Genuine spirituality is an aspect of the collective unconscious and is independent of childhood programming and the individual's cultural or educational background. Thus, if self-exploration reaches sufficient depth, spiritual elements emerge spontaneously into consciousness." The therapeutic methods of Jung and Grof do not place very much emphasis on rational understanding. They commit themselves to an active transformation of one's innermost being. This occurs during a direct experience of these deep layers of the psyche, which are interpreted as an autonomous, second personality. The object of this is to help the client come in contact with these deep layers of the unconscious, and utilize the ancient wisdom that is slumbering there.

The important aspect of Alf's treatment was the fact that he *accepted* the clients' quest. He felt that men and women always have, always will, and always should seek to rise above their limitations, toward a spiritual experience. He realized that the root of the alcohol/narcotics problem is the fact that our shallow Western culture has failed completely, as far as meeting this fundamental human need is concerned. Not until we recognize the significance of non-ordinary states of consciousness, can we help people satisfy their spiritual needs without chemical means.

Alf refused to put labels on people—"alcoholics," "drug addicts"—which could be difficult for them to get rid of. To him, the clients, with their quests, were often the most valuable people. He said, "I encourage your search. But I would like to help you to take a better path." Self-knowledge, meditation, music, communion with nature, opening up to others, often a complete change of environment. Never going back to the streets. "You don't enter the lion's den with a raw beef sandwich in your hand!" Alf often said.

This was a happy period in Australia. I lived out in the woods, an hour-and-a-half by car from Melbourne. If I were awake by six in the morning, it happened that I saw kangaroos bounding away with their tremendous leaps. At night, in the headlights of my car, I sometimes caught a glimpse of a koala bear up in a tree. Outside my window I could inspect a whole flock of Australian king parrots with their red and green plumage. In the nearby field sat hundreds of chalk-white cockatoos, with yellow crests on their heads. In the closest tree there often sat a kookaburra that laughs at you with its "human" laughter.

° ° °

I have a new dream. I am sitting with a woman and a little child. In front of me a Tyrannosaurus is roaring. Various colored lightbulbs are fastened to its body. The woman and the child are frightened. I say, "Sit still!" I feel that I can control the animal with my gaze and my voice.

The animal has a bow and arrow, which it aims at me. Shoots but misses. Purely symbolically, I throw a stone back. The animal hardly feels it on its body. Then I go over to the Tyrannosaurus with an outstretched hand.

This dream initiates another inner journey. Who is the Tyrannosaurus? Inside me.

I experience the same transit. I tremble and shake. And then it feels as if I am leaving my body. This time directly into the "other world." This alien landscape. These strange trees. They have leaves and flowers as big as plate glass windows. And the strange animals. In shapes and colors that I have never seen on Earth. There are no buildings here, only columns and pillars. But, at the same time as I say this, it's as if everything is indoors.

This *is* another world. But I know that I have been here before. Not during these "journeys" of mine. But earlier. As a child, perhaps, during deliriums of fever. Or even further back?

I say to Anne, who is lying beside me with a writing pad and pencil, "I am in another world. But I have been here before."

At the same moment as I say this, the pictures disappear. The Luminous Being is standing there, signalling, I mustn't speak. I think: is it really so fragile? I say to Anne, "I don't want to speak."

I lie and wait. Pictures return. I become irritated. I want to speak, have her with me. I say, "Of course I'm going to speak." The pictures disappear. I wait. They do not reappear.

This is becoming ridiculous. I say finally, "I don't want to speak." I can't be in both worlds at the same time.

So I lie there silently, looking at the pictures before my inner eye. I think: So these pictures are *inside* me. They are not memories, something I remember from this life. They are not dreams. They are far more realistic and substantial. But they are in me. Are they fantasies? But what is fantasy? Where does that come from?

Suddenly I am standing before a bridge of light. A bridge of light that goes up to higher spheres. I hear a voice saying, "Follow me!" I catch a glimpse of the Luminous Being up there. What is this? Am I to leave the earthly sphere? Is this what I am being asked to do, when I am to accompany you?

Perhaps I can leave the earthly sphere. But this includes Anne. I am not prepared to forsake Anne. I feel her warmth beside me. I cannot exist without Anne. We belong together, we still have so much to give each other. I touch her gently. Then the entire bridge of light collapses inside my head and turns into chaos.

I let go of Anne and curl up by myself, pulling the blanket tightly around me, encapsulating myself in myself. The journey continues.

I am in Africa. In a village of straw huts. I am black. A chieftain, I think. Around me there are many men, children and women. The sand is red. The clothes colorful. The adults sit plaiting twigs. The children are playing on me. I remain for a while.

Now I am in a greener landscape. I am sitting on the veranda of my manor house, looking out over the valley, a beautiful, undulating valley. Green fields and tall, magnificent leafy trees. It could be in England, or in France perhaps. A woman is sitting opposite me. An elegant, beautiful woman, with grey hair and a finely-chiseled face. She is my wife. I call her "The Duchess." We have had a long and happy life together. I love her. I have loved her all my life. It is good just sitting with her on this fine veranda. I look at the white, ornate railing. We belong to each other. I have led a busy life, with considerable power, responsibility and authority. She has stood by my side. It is good to rest. We smile at each other. I hold out my hand. She grasps it. A picture of blissful peace.

New experiences. Now I am a young girl. In my teens. I am in love, it is a beautiful experience. I am waiting for my first boyfriend. I will make love to him when he comes. I feel the euphoria of expectation... I lie there for a long time. I am naked in bed and happen to touch myself. I am astonished to discover that I am a man.

It was an enrichment to experience the way a young woman feels.

° ° °

Again I must ask, what are these experiences? They are so life-like. So realistic. What is reality? These pictures and experiences are *more* intense than what we usually call reality. I am present in them even more strongly. There can be no doubt that there are other "worlds," in other states of consciousness. *Being* this young woman is not something I am imagining. I *live* being her. I believe our consciousness is limited by our body. When we leave the body, as I felt I did, the consciousness is expanded. We experience realms other than the ones we are in contact with every day.

It is tempting to ask: Have I ever been a young girl, a woman, at some time in a previous life? Is this what I am re-experiencing? Has my consciousness been connected with previous lives?

If so, do I have the reminiscences of these lives in me? Is it true that I can come in contact with them during my special journeys? And why do I experience precisely the things that I do? Who determines *what* I shall experience? Is there any connection with where I find myself today, perhaps? With my situation in *this* life? And what does it *mean* for me to have these experiences? One thing is certain: there is considerable energy connected with these experiences. It comes as a relief when the energy is discharged. And the discharge occurs precisely because the experience is so real. This is not something that I *remember*. But something that is really *happening*, here and now. Throughout my life I have had problems with my neck and shoulders. Stiff muscles. After my experiences during the previous journey, the stiffness has gone. And I feel more confident.

I make these reflections after I have come back. While the journey was in progress, I *experienced* it most of all. Then experiencing is enough. I become aware of one very important thing: As far as the essence of things is concerned, we are unable to understand. We can only experience. This is the way it is. Experiencing is enough. Because an understanding that is different and deeper than intellectual understanding emerges from this.

° ° °

But the journey was not over. The most violent, the most shocking part was yet to come. I experience that something is tearing and pulling at me. It feels like a black shadow. No, more than a shadow. A gigantic black shape. It is pulling at me in order to take me with it.

To go with it means death. More than death, it means surrendering to "Evil." It is "Evil" that I am struggling against. This figure is "Evil." I feel it, I know it, it is "Evil" that wants to get hold of me. I seize Anne's arm. "Evil" takes hold of my shoulders and tries to pull me away. It pulls me with all its might. I resist.

"It's up there!" I say to Anne. "It wants to take me."

This is not something that occurs quickly. It happens very slowly. It lasts for an hour, perhaps even longer. It pulls. I resist. I catch a glimpse of Anne's eyes in the darkness. They are expressionless. "Evil" is here in the room. This time the "everyday" reality and the "other" reality are present in the same room. There is no doubt, "Evil" wants to get hold of me. It wants to tear me away from life, which is Anne. What kind of force is this? It feels as if it is physical. But at the same time it is taking place inside me, at another level.

It is a silent struggle. I resist with all my might. For a long time it is a deadlock. Neither of us gains the upper hand. I know that I mustn't allow it to gain power over me.

Suddenly I hate Anne. She comes and goes and is so unstable! Why can't she go forever, or stay? I have an impulse to kill her. I think: She doesn't love me! She is unfaithful to me! She is lying to me! I hear myself asking: "Do you know what love is?" Criticism is implied by the question.

Anne thinks it over for a long time before she answers. Her voice is gentle. "Yes, I know what love is."

To my amazement, the room lights up when she says this. The room was in complete darkness. For an instant it is completely light. I can see every detail in here. "Evil" releases its hold. I sink back, exhausted.

Anne gets up and goes in front of the bed to the bathroom. There is a light around her naked body. What do I see? Is it her aura?

The light disappears with her when she goes out. Again the bedroom is completely dark. She comes back, and again

I see the ring of light around her. The light is more golden than white. It extends perhaps a foot-and-a-half away from her body, and surrounds her completely.

Anne crawls under the blanket, the light disappears. I look at this extraordinary person. I am aware of the fact that she has psychic ability! But such a fine Aura! I have never seen a human aura before. Now I have seen it with my own eyes! They have been opened, they can see something they usually do not see.

I love Anne. I have surrendered myself to her, unconditionally. This is the first year of our marriage. She has difficulties with being married, says it gives her claustrophobia, makes her feel trapped. She has problems flying in planes and riding in elevators. I want so much to help her, if she will give me a chance. Now I try to experience her, what it is like to be her. Anne and I are able to communicate in other ways than with words, even across the Atlantic. Become aware of what is happening to the other. Now I experience her fear. But I don't know what she is afraid of. And I experience her despair. When we got married, we wrote our own vows to each other. One of them was that we would encourage and support the growth and development of the other. I want to support her, even if it means her saying goodbye to me.

° ° °

The struggle is over. The Evil is gone. Anne tells me that she saw the Evil in the room. Like a black shadow above me. It resembled a horrible bird, she says. A gigantic raven. She felt that it filled the room, and does not doubt that it was present. She saw the struggle. The air had been charged.

She says that in order to help me, she surrounded me with light, but that she felt powerless.

What did this "Evil" want with me? Did it really want to drag me away from life? From Anne? Into *its* realm? Which was something quite different from the promised land I had glimpsed into the last time.

Now, afterwards, I realize that these experiences are symbolic. But while they are taking place they seem real. At any rate, it makes me ask if "Evil" really exists. In material disguises. Like a force of nature, perhaps. Is it the dark side of the Creator? To say that Evil arises only from fear or an unhappy childhood seems naive. I experienced Evil as coming from a different dimension, as a universal force. Evil as opposed to Good, darkness as opposed to light. How far along the way does Evil rule humankind? Or has it been created by humanity itself?

I believe that we *must* bring Evil out into the open and fight it. There is no use pretending it isn't there. Denying its existence. Repressing it. If we are to make progress, we must integrate even that into our personality, make friends with it, without succumbing to it. I also believe that love becomes superficial if we haven't had a duel with Evil.

According to a venerable Catholic priest, "The power of evil is chained. A chained dog cannot bite you unless you go up to it."

A pretty speech, but is it that simple? When we see all the evil that it is taking place in the world, and we feel the impulses in ourselves, mustn't we admit that evil is a reality which we must learn to live with? As Jung says, we must neither "succumb" to evil nor good, nor allow ourselves to be seduced by the opposition between good and evil. I quote from his autobiography, *Memories, Dreams, Reflections*: "The individual who wishes to have an answer to the problem of Evil as it is posed today, has need, first and foremost, of *self-knowledge*, that is, the utmost possible knowledge of his own wholeness. He must know relentlessly how much good he can do, and what crimes he is capable of, and must beware of regarding the one as real and the other as illusion. Both are elements within his nature, and both are bound to come to light in him, should he wish—as he ought—to live without self-deception or self—illusion."

° ° °

I say to Anne, "After this round I feel completely exhausted."

"You've had a tough time of it."

"That I went about with all this 'evil.' These 'powers of darkness,' to use an old-fashioned expression."

Anne looks at me for a moment. Then she takes my hand. "Come," she says, and leads me over to the mirror.

"Look at him in there." Anne points. "What do you see?"

"I see...," I hesitate. "I see... I don't like what I see."

"I like it," Anne says. "Take a good look at this wise, charming man."

"I can't stare at myself this way."

"Look at him. No, not at me, at him!"

"I can't!" I say despairingly.

"Look him in the eye. What do you see?"

"I don't know what I see."

"Say to him...," her voice becomes intimate, "I love you."

"But I don't."

"How can you expect anyone else to love you if you don't do it yourself?"

"That is true."

"How can you love me," she continues, "if you don't love you?"

"I don't know."

"Say it now."

"I can't make myself do it. Can you?"

Anne leans forward, stares intently at herself in the mirror. "You there, I love you." She laughs. "Now it's your turn."

I lean forward. Am unable to say anything.

"Be brave now."

"I love you... you idiot!"

"No, not idiot. Say it properly."

I look myself in the eye, say calmly, "I love you."

"Bravo!"

"I thought you were making fun of me."

"Fun? No. Now say it every morning."

° ° °

Anne and I go for a walk along the river. It has just stopped raining. The sun is peeping out. The grassy bank is steaming. I remember this wonderful fragrance from my childhood: sun on the soil after the rain.

I take Anne by the hand. "I feel like a plant," I say, "that has been yanked up out of the ground and had the dirt shaken off its roots."

"Then it has to put down roots again," Anne says.

Only now does it occur to me: I walked toward that Tyrannosaurus with an outstretched hand. Strange how the experiences in the dreams and during the inner journeys are interconnected. Yes, it is a process.

The desire for knowledge is, to me, the karma which leads from previous lives into this life and on to future lives. In my case it must have been, primarily, a passionate urge towards understanding which brought about my birth.

The meaning of my existence, as I interpret it, is that life has addressed a question to me,—a question which perhaps occupied me or my ancestors from a previous life, and which they could not answer.

C.G. Jung

Anne is an American. I am Norwegian. Periodically we live apart. Now we are together again, after having been separated from each other for six weeks. Anne has been working on her doctoral thesis in psychology. I have done my work in Norway. The separation has "made the hearts grow fonder."

She has picked me up at the airport. In the car, we sit with a warm hand on each others' thigh. At home, inside the door, she takes off her coat. I kiss her. She unbuttons her dress. We make our way to the living room. Our clothes like blotches of color behind us. We make love on the couch, on the floor. Ravenously and happily.

° ° °

I must go on. In my search. What is driving me? The curiosity of the scholar? Yes. But there is something more. I feel it as an imperative, a command. There is something greater than I am. That is ruling over me. It is as if this has been planned. This is the way it is supposed to be. This is what I am supposed to do. And now this message: Tell!

During this period I undertake three inner journeys.

On the first journey a flock of little green creatures takes me through the passageway. Everything seems to happen slowly, ominously. I come to a strange room—pure science fiction—the interior of a spaceship. Why not a flying saucer? The whole interior is made of metal. There are pipes everywhere. I am lying on my back in the middle of the room.

Around me it is teeming with strange, silent little genderless men. They are not human beings. They are dressed in the same uniform, mostly green, a little blue. Slowly they come closer. Threatening? It is not pleasant. What is happening to me? I do not want to be afraid. I am willing to give in. What strange creatures. They lean over me, but they don't touch me. They are merely transmitting something to me, some rays. I don't know what they are. Is it in order to break down my human resistance, all the tensions in my body? Perhaps they are transmitting this "something" in order to make me relax. God knows, I've been so tense. The creatures parade around me. Almost respectfully. I dare say, they wish me well.

I am ready to continue on my journey. Suddenly it strikes me like a bolt of lightning: My father!

I see him sitting before me as an old man, in the chair in the nursing home where he spent his final years. This really happened, in the everyday reality. I had been hurling abuse at him, reproaching him for clipping my wings ever since I was little. A hatred for him had welled up inside me. With roots in ancient jealousy, perhaps, because I felt that he was to blame for my not having had a more intimate contact with my distant, beloved mother.

My father and I were never on the same wavelength. I felt that he wanted to hinder me in my growth, mold me into the life *he* envisioned. During all those years I had avoided a confrontation with him. Not until he was old did I unleash the storm. I should have been adult enough to have avoided it, but it welled up inside me. I couldn't resist.

He was sitting there, alone, bewildered, stripped of his guiding principles. I remember having thought: Where is the faith he had in God? I had hurled abuse at him. Finally he had said these words: "But have you no mercy?" No, I had no mercy. I *had* to get the hatred out of me. The hatred that was so much greater because I knew that I had once loved him.

And now, in my journey, I relive this scene. The film runs slowly. I had no mercy. I had no mercy for that old man. I try to explain it away to myself, find excuses. But one sentence keeps coming back again and again: He was a person in an extreme spiritual crisis, who was asking for mercy, and I had none.

Now I reach out my hand to him, but he does not move. He just looks at me. Not reproachfully, nothing, his eyes are expressionless. The fear is gone, the anxiety is gone, the despair is gone. His gaze is completely neutral. He just sits and waits, as he looks straight through me.

What kind of person am I? A heart of stone. The man with the heart of stone. I cannot live with this man. My father disappears. The Luminous Being is standing there. I say, "Take my life! I offer my life. I give my life in order to make up for this."

But the Luminous Being does not want my life. This is probably too simple. I *must* accept, I *must* face up to it, the heart of stone. I *must* learn to live with this man. But it is impossible. I whisper, "Please take my life. Please."

Slowly it subsides. The baying of the hounds. Then something surprising happens. I am at Court. The ceiling is high. The walls and floor are covered with rugs. They appear to be Caucasian. In the middle of the room there is a podium, two steps up. There stands the king, clad in a magnificent blue robe with gilt edges. There are many people around him. This must be several hundred years ago. The king gives an order. Two men seize me, remove my shirt and start to beat me with a stick.

This time it isn't suffering, it is punishment. And I stand the pain, blows on my back, not my shoulders and neck. I feel it is just. I accept it patiently. Want it to continue until I have received my share. The king is not hostile. He is a fair king, and I accept him.

The Court vanishes. The Luminous Being is standing there, and says, "You must have mercy on yourself."

There is a landslide inside me. The blocks of stone melt. There is a lump in my throat. My eyes are filled with tears. "Thank you," I whisper. "Thank you."

° ° °

My mother said, "One begins by loving one's parents and ends by forgiving them." They are both gone. I have long since forgiven. And asked them to forgive me. I believe they can bestow this forgiveness from where they are now.

I also regard what happened between my father and me at that time as a link in the process. The fact that everything has a meaning, *stands* for something. In truth, he made his contribution with his pain, the good, warmhearted person that he was.

I send a friendly thought to the little green creatures, who sent this "something" through me, and helped me to open up.

After this journey I feel a deep reconciliation with my father. I see him in a new light. See aspects of him that I had forgotten or was unaware of. It was not easy for *him*. He lived for 25 years with my mother's mother in the house. She had to be nursed around the clock. This sapped most of my mother's strength. I wonder how much was left for him.

I have also come to a new reconciliation with myself.

° ° °

The next inner journey appears to be devoted to the Duchess. I meet her early. We are sitting on the veranda as before. The sun is warm, even though it is late in November. Her face is turned a little to one side. I see her beautiful profile. She is more pensive than usual. I read her face. We married early. Her face is my best book.

I don't know which century this is. I don't think it is very long ago. She is wearing a white blouse and a green skirt that reaches to her ankles.

Normally I feel such peace when I am with her. It is bliss to have this feeling of belonging, without question marks, beyond any doubt. But today there is a shadow over the valley. I have a premonition of something, I don't know what.

Anne is playing Bach for me. I say, "It sounds so sad." She is about to protest, but I ask her to turn it off. All the music she has played today has sounded like funeral dirges to my ears.

I close my eyes, go back to the Duchess. This is just something I call her. I am not a Duke. Although, why not? I rule over much land and many people. The Duchess has always stood by my side. Her strength... I don't know what I would have been without her. I realize this now, in my old age. My gratitude is great. Nothing is too good for her. She is not only my wife and mistress. She is my best friend.

I discuss every question with her. I say, "I have prayed to God and tried to speak with Him. But He turns a deaf ear."

She replies, "If you throw all the china on the floor and break it, then He will speak to us."

"But I have inherited the china from my mother!"

"Then you must choose: God or the china."

"Mother or the china," I say.

"Mother or God, perhaps," she laughs.

"If I believed..."

"Abraham believed," she looks at me, "when he went to sacrifice Isaac. What is china compared to a son?"

I look at her thoughtfully. "But Abraham had received the message from God."

"Perhaps God is speaking through me."

I think: No, I will not sacrifice the china.

I sit looking at her, her warm smile, her classic features. How stylish and elegant. I say, "After all these years, I desire you as much as ever."

She looks at me mischievously. Then she lifts her skirt. "Come, then!"

But I do not come. I remain sitting and look at her. My heart is heavy. I don't understand this. I look at her with all my senses. So that I shall never forget her. The calm brown eyes, the straight nose, the soft wide mouth, the narrow cheeks, the high forehead. This beautiful, aristocratic face that I love. Around her eyes there is a network of wrinkles. Every line in this face tells of our life together, our good life.

She looks at me questioningly. I shake my head slowly.

The shadow in the valley has come closer. Suddenly I am alone on the veranda. I hear church bells. More and more I feel that something is wrong. People come up the valley, a whole procession. A funeral procession. I am filled with great unrest. I exclaim, "Oh God, please help me!"

I open my eyes. Anne is sitting there. Looking at me in amazement. I say to her, "You know, I think she is dead."

"Who?"

"The Duchess. I think I have lost her. Oh God!"

Anne places her hand over mine, says tenderly, "Tell me."

"I loved her so dearly. Such a long life is needed for that. To think that I understand this."

I start to cry. Anne puts her arm around me.

"I can only love one. I loved her. But now she is dead. I remember it. I was born with this grief. Now I understand it. I haven't understood it before."

I am sobbing.

"To think that the sorrow was so great. Oh God, this is a totally different dimension."

Anne holds me in her arms.

"Experiencing this is the most important thing that has ever happened to me." I wipe away my tears. "You see, all my life I have been so sad. I was born with this sadness. It was because I lost her. I never recovered from this grief."

Anne cradles me in her arms. I cry.

"I couldn't bear it. I took it with me to the grave. So *this* was the meaning of this life. To recover from this sorrow."

I am unable to stop crying. Every vent is open. Anne says that I cried for an hour.

° ° °

The next day Anne and I talk about yesterday's experience. She says, "Do you believe that she is *real*, this Duchess? That she was from a previous life?"

I think it over. "I don't know what to think. My feelings were so intense."

"I have never seen anyone cry like that."

"You know, it really doesn't make any difference," I say. "The most important thing is that I experienced it."

"This is true."

"I am so relieved. I have really gotten rid of a great sorrow."

"You look much happier."

"I've continually gone about feeling sad and melancholy. Now it is gone. This is so strange."

There is a pause. We sit lost in thought. I study Anne's face.

"It's funny," I say, "but I see the Duchess in you."

Anne looks at me silently.

"You have the same air about you. The same expression in your eyes."

"Have you seen this in your other women?"

"Yes, in the love of my youth. But I made a mess of that."

Anne sits without speaking for a while. "Do you remember my telling you that I had a kind of vision?" she says. "The first month we were together?"

"I've forgotten the details," I say. "Tell me again."

"You came out into the kitchen and put your arms around me. Then I had a strange "playback." I experienced that I was in an old house. I was standing in the pantry, wearing a long crinoline dress. We had guests in the dining room. I had gone to get some food, and you came looking for me. You put your arms around me affectionately in order to comfort me because you would soon be going away."

"In your vision, as well?"

"Yes."

"We were married, then?"

"We'd been married for many years. You were a governor or something like that, and you travelled a lot. Then something happened. I believe it was sad."

I look at her. "So perhaps there was something remaining from that time, that we were supposed to finish?"

"You mean, since the two of us had to meet each other?"

"Something we were supposed to learn. Both of us. I was supposed to recover from the grief. What do you think you were supposed to learn?"

"What freedom is," Anne replies.

° ° °

Two or three years after I had been to Esalen for the first time, it occurred to me that I had to go there again. I didn't exactly know why. To be sure, the lecturers were good. In addition to Stanislav Grof, they included leading people in their respective fields like Fritjof Capra, David Steindl-Rast, Ralph Metzner, Richard Price, Sogyol Rinpoche Lama, and others. But I had been working with Grof's methods to such an extent that, from a purely professional point of view, there was no real necessity for a new stay. Nevertheless, unknown to me, I felt that I had to go.

I was admitted to a new, four-week seminar, and one day I was again sitting on the floor in "The Big Room," with thirty people from all over the world. Largely psychologists.

At one time, Esalen had been an Indian dwelling place and sacrificial site. Intense mystical forces prevail there. I was to feel this. It is a long way from civilization, all the way down by the shoreline of the Pacific.

A brook runs through a ravine filled with exotic plants. The buildings are placed among ancient trees. The sun seldom stops shining. Day and night, the sea rolls in and out in heavy swells. During my first visit, in a session on non-ordinary state of unconsciousness, I lay listening to the ocean. The sound of the water pounding against the cliffs rose and fell. My breathing fell into the same rhythm—long, calm movements. And I experienced that I *was* the ocean.

Many vegetables, herbs, fruits, etc., are grown organically on the spot. The bread is baked there. Springing from the rocks, hot sulphur water collects in small pools—hot tubs. It is wonderful to sit there, and gaze out over the ocean, looking at the sunsets in the evenings. Or at night. Esalen is so far away from neon-lit cities that Heaven can display its myriad stars without interference.

The first morning, I let my eyes wander from participant to participant as we sat on pillows around the blue carpet. Facing me was an unusually beautiful woman, with brown, mournful eyes. Our eyes met. Something happened there, between our eyes. When we stood up for the first break, I went over to her and said, "I have come for you."

After a week, we rented a little house for ourselves in the mountains above the Institute. "Roof-top" became our first love nest, with a view over the jagged, steep, green-brown-red California coast and the Pacific. We *had* to join forces. We had no other choice.

When the seminar was over, I flew back to Norway. Three weeks later we celebrated Christmas in her house on the eastern coast of the U.S., and started our life together. A year later we were married, even though neither of us was looking for marriage. We have both been married twice before. Both times briefly for her. The opposite for me.

Since our meeting, we have lived for a while in Norway, but mostly in the U.S. I call myself a "monthly commuter" across the Atlantic. Gradually it became apparent that Anne had to remain in her own homeland—partly because of her work and partly because she is so strongly attached to her family.

Anne is an excellent psychologist. She knows that professional competence is not enough to heal someone. Love and care are the primary factors that stimulate the patient's own healing mechanism. The idea is not to force the patient into the pattern which the psychologist believes is correct, but to understand that we are all in the process of learning the teachings that have been arranged for us by God, or our destiny—where we now find ourselves in our process.

Anne is a good listener. People simply open up. She gives them warmth, understanding, confidence, contact. This woman is not afraid of flying.

But Anne is two people. She was born under the sign of Gemini—the twins. The other side of her is anxious and insecure. I once experienced this side of her as a lost child. In an authoritarian home, she learned early that it paid to please, and her mind had adapted itself to pleasing others. An important part of herself, of her emotional life, was unable to develop. Now, this part is fighting for air.

Throughout her life, Anne has been greatly dominated by her father. He started with two empty hands and became rich. In his eightieth year he controls and rules his family of two generations. He respects me because I have been the chairman of the board of so many companies. One day I told him that I had backed out in order to become a writer. I waited for his disapproval. Instead he said, "Well, perhaps you can earn even more money at that. McDonald was a pensioner when he started with his hamburgers."

° ° °

My third inner journey begins early in the evening. We have gone to bed, as always lying close together in one big bed, under one big coverlet and always naked. Anything else is inconceivable to us. We also have a principle which we think is a good one: whenever one of us is really wanting, the other is ready to volunteer. It works both ways.

Anne has reluctantly spent the evening looking over some investments. I can feel that for once her knees are cold. I say, "I'll warm you." I think: Cold knees are a symbol of the business world.

Anne is tired, and after a while she falls asleep. I'm lying by myself in the darkness, listening to the silence, breathing deeply and waiting for the journey to begin. Many weeks have passed since our last passionate reunion. We have long since returned to everyday life. Anne has been interviewing people as a link in the work on her doctoral thesis: people who have had near-death experiences. I have been studying Jung, Grof, Michael Grosso and others who are occupied with human consciousness. And working on my book.

Each of these inner journeys has provided me with new insight, and also released me from a burden. I go to this research with a critical sense and skepticism, but I cannot explain away what I feel. My emotions, the way I am, are a barometer. I must believe in my emotions. They do not lie. It feels good just to be alive.

In this book I am trying to give an account of my experiences with as few explanations as possible, in order that the readers may take part in them and, I hope, experience something themselves. However, there is one insurmountable problem: the fact that the language I am able to use consists only of words. The experiences during these journeys are so overwhelming that it is difficult to put them into words. I realize that language is not the true "language." Language has been invented by human beings for practical reasons, to enable us to communicate with each other. But these experiences go beyond that part of the human condition for which we have words. Behind the language there is something else, the real thing. Words are only symbols of this. In fact, words may cut one off from the experience they represent. I believe there is a "language" without words.

Poetry is perhaps that which comes closest. William Blake expresses his vision of cosmic unity as follows:

Awake! Awake oh sleeper of the land of shadows,
 wake! expand!
I am in you and you in me, mutual in love...
Fibers of love from man to man...
Lo! we are one.

What I am engaged in is not a joking matter. Each journey is a shattering experience, an encounter with what Arthur Koestler called the elevated, the "tragic" dimension. This, as opposed to the "trivial," everyday dimension, the business acumen to which we were asked to devote ourselves. After having visited this elevated, "tragic" dimension, it may be difficult to reconcile oneself to the trivial dimension again. So many things appear in a different light. All the "entertainment" that we are inundated with, for example. Or the fact that people are so greedy for power and wealth. It seems incomprehensible that they are able to devote so much energy and strength to this. It becomes downright ludicrous.

Violence is experienced as a form of blindness, to be dazzled by destructive forces, to be in their power, abandoned to them, unable to *see*. The blind needs help to see, to bring out "The Evil," and fight with it. Perhaps, one day, to understand. We must protect ourselves against the violence. But we cannot punish a man simply because he is blind.

° ° °

The time has come. I feel that the journey is beginning. Shall I wake Anne? She has had a busy day. I let her sleep. She is lying with her back to me. I feel the warmth of her body. I place my hand on her hip. She is sleeping soundly.

I go through the passage. The familiar pictures. I think: This is boring. I would much rather be with Anne. What am I doing here alone? I want to escape into her arms, embrace her.

But I lie still, content myself with my hand against her skin.

Then, ahead of me, I see a shining stairway. It goes straight up from the field where I find myself. Disappears further than I can see. A figure, clad in white, is standing high up on the stairs. It is the Luminous Being. She signals to me that I am supposed to climb the stairs, accompany her.

I hesitate. It seems like an eternity. On one side, the stairway bathed in light, the waiting figure. On the other side, Anne. I understand that I must choose. If I go up the stairs, I must renounce Anne. What does the Luminous Being up there expect of me? I don't understand. Only realize that it is a request to be followed blindly.

No, I am not ready this time, either. I love Anne. I feel her warm skin under my hand. I move my hand. An uncontrollable desire wells up inside me, to make love to her. Penetrate her, be one with her. No, I am not ready to leave the "lust of the flesh," if this is what I am being asked to do.

I do not want to awaken her. This desire, again I experience it as the primitive force. Man's desire for woman's sex. Woman's craving for man's. Just beneath the respectable, proper surface lies this primitive force. I realize how important it is to integrate this into the personality as well. How strong it is, and how easily things may go wrong if we repress it or it goes astray. And I understand the importance of loyalty and fidelity if this force is to function constructively, and not destructively, in a relationship of love. Give nourishment to a richer emotional spectrum.

I think about my own childhood and growth, with sexual fears, feelings of guilt and shame, and how many years it has taken me to be free, to release this primitive force within me for pleasure and pride, tenderness and delight.

I lie there, aware of the impulses and the thoughts. Free, truly free, I wrote before, is a question of an *inner* freedom. To be able to allow my thoughts and imagination to wander freely, without restrictions that have been built in by others or by myself. First of all, it takes courage to dare to stand face-to-face with one's own thoughts. Not shove them away or embellish them, not even to oneself. Again I experience the way this can settle in the body. Not only as stiff muscles. It affects the digestion. It affects the chemistry. All kinds of illness may arise from it.

It occurs to me: "If you want to be free, then you must be free of guilt." Yes, this must be true.

Anne is sound asleep. I am longing for her desperately. But I still don't want to wake her. I think: "This longing is also a lack of freedom." I am longing to thrust my face between her thighs. To gaze into those beautiful eyes. To stroke her body with my hand. I am longing to nestle against her, closely, closely, feel the warmth—forget... forget. Oh Lord! Is it my mother? Am I longing for my mother? What kind of bondage is this? Is a longing for my mother at the bottom of my need for a woman? My inability to be alone? That I am clinging to Anne more than is good for her, while it is best for her that I let her go? That I am clinging to her for fear of losing her, pure and simple? That I am trying to possess her. What lack of freedom!!! Thank you, dear God, for this insight! Never again will I cling to any woman! Come as a free man! Give of myself, love unconditionally. Oh God, now I have rid myself of a "tether" inside my head! What a relief! Oh, it feels good!

After a while I, too, fall asleep.

° ° °

Freedom.

Anne has a desperate need to be free in *this* life. Was the Duchess, in reality, so unfulfilled and so lacking in freedom?

And I? I dare say I was supposed to learn more than recovering from my grief. I was supposed to learn how to stand on my own two feet. Without the Duchess.

Now I understand why, at this time, Anne and I both received, or chose, the life we were experiencing. And why we had to meet each other.

Is there someone who still doesn't believe in a pattern? Or Providence? *Something* is going on.

The ultimate reality is not to be found at the plane of everyday ego-centered experience, as we tend to think, but at the level of the unconscious and the archetypes.

C.G. Jung

Anne's doctoral thesis is about people who have had so-called near-death experiences (NDE), that is to say, people who have briefly experienced death and have come back again. It now seems obvious that millions of people have had such experiences in the United States alone. Most of them describe the same things: going through a tunnel, the light at the other end, an overwhelming light that is experienced as love, eternal, all-embracing peace and love. Being one with this light is experienced as meeting God. They also describe meeting deceased loved ones who tell them that the time is not yet ripe and send them back again.

People who have had such experiences do not doubt that a different dimension exists, and that what has happened to them is most genuine and very real.

The usual view is that these people have become more harmonious afterwards. They acquire new values. Money, power, careers, earthly and material possessions mean less to them. They are more concerned with spiritual values. They often recall feelings of immortality, the suspension of time and space. The encounter with death expands their spirituality, but apparently not in a conventional religious sense. This is as true of atheists as it is for the faithful. Religious distinctions cease to exist. A spiritual unity appears to arise, independent of one's previous faith. Little or no importance is placed on the concept of sin. The encounter with light eliminates self-righteousness and condemnation. Most people say that love is the only thing that matters.

Gradually Anne has come to the conclusion that it is not always easy for these people—after a glimpse of Eternity—to return to a life they may not want. It can be difficult to readjust to the daily grind, and all of its superficial, stressful triviality. Some are completely incapable of watching television and are repelled by any portrayal of violence. For many, the worst thing is a feeling of loneliness, the inability to talk about their experience, because no one understands or is willing to believe, not even those closest to them. So they remained silent. Today it appears to be easier, however, as a result of all the books that have been written on the subject and the fact that professionals, like Anne, have started support groups.

Researchers have found that there are significant parallels between NDE and similar states of non-ordinary consciousness. Not only may the experience itself be identical, but also an intense feeling of heightened reality. They believe that the same chemical reactions occur in the brain during a near-death experience, as for example during hyperventilation. In one case, a patient's blood oxygen level, measured at the exact moment of his near-death experience, was much above normal.* (We will return to the subject of NDE in the second part of this book.)

I am very familiar with the lonely feeling of such extraordinary experiences. There are a few initiates whom one may talk with. Naturally enough, it is difficult for the uninitiated to comprehend.

Because there *are* two "worlds." If I try to explain things from the "other world," I can tell by the expression of the listener that he or she is thinking: "He's probably out his

---

*Michael Sabom: *Recollections of Death. A Medical Investigation.* Harper and Row, New York, 1982.

mind." Or else the comment, "They're only hallucinations." Whatever. The word "hallucination" comes from "alucinare," which means "to wander in the mind;" that is to say, "to undertake inner journeys in the consciousness." It does not mean seeing "unreal" phenomena.... Picture a literal-minded flatlander telling an astronaut that the world's not round.

I don't know anyone who explains this feeling of loneliness better than Jung: "Loneliness does not come from having no people about one, but from being unable to communicate the things that seem important to oneself, or from holding certain views which others find inadmissible."

° ° °

Anne and I have again been apart for several weeks. She was supposed to have taken a trip to Norway, but it was Father's Day, so she couldn't come. Now together again in the house by the river, we put our arms around each other.

"Love is a strange thing," she says, "that can cause so much pain."

"And joy," I say.

"Where does it come from? Where is it located?"

She holds me tight. I see fear in her eyes. "Your eyes are afraid," I say. "You can tell the truth. You needn't be afraid."

"I felt I never could when I was growing up. I was afraid of what might happen." She hesitates. "The truth is... I have to be free."

Turning it over in one's mind is one thing, but confronting it, facing up to it.... I thought I was prepared. But I wasn't.

She continues: "I knew, the first year, that we *had* to be together. There was no other way. But when we got married, it became destructive and not constructive for me."

"It was the other way around for me," I say.

"Then the claustrophobia came back. Apparently I can never stay married for more than three months."

"Perhaps we could find the roots of your claustrophobia together."

"I don't know. Now I have this feeling that I must go away again. Be free. I've always been like this. After three years I have to break off a relationship. And move. Sell my house. It is as if something changes gears inside me. I *have* to move on."

"You must do whatever you feel like," I say.

She says, "It's hard. Because I love you. Never have I been so close."

We sit silently, holding each other by the hand. I say, "Perhaps you're confusing inner freedom with external freedom. It is possible to be free, free inside, and belong to each other. I believe that only then can we be free."

"I know this in theory. But the way I feel now, I'm no good to anyone. Not creative. I have everything. I have you. You have all the qualities I desire in a man. And yet I must be free."

I think: This is not the time to feel sorry for myself.

She looks at me. "You once said that I was a wild bird that had landed in your garden. Can you let the wild bird fly?"

I do not answer right away. I have shared every thought, every emotion with her. She is my best friend. She has opened new rooms inside me, rooms I didn't know existed. Painful thoughts rush through my mind: She doesn't really love me! Perhaps she has found someone else! If she loves me, why can't she work on her freedom with me?

She says, "Is there anything I can do for you?"

I am ashamed of my thoughts. But I got married in order to have a companion, a partner to share the rest of my life with. I am no longer young. Then I have to smile. Was it a new Duchess that I wanted? The Duchess' wings hadn't appeared to be clipped at the time. But had I ever asked myself what *she* wanted to do with her life, other than be a support to me?

"Is being married what you are incapable of?" I ask. "We can get a divorce... and continue as before."

She says, "I must have time to find myself."

"What do you mean by time?"

"A couple of months, at any rate."

"And after that?"

She looks away. "I don't know. Of course I want us to remain friends. All I know is that now I have to be free." The tears run down her cheeks.

"Don't be afraid," I say. "I love you. Deeply enough to let the wild bird fly."

"Thank you for understanding."

Do I understand? A part of me understands. But another part is unable to comprehend it. I think: What does she want? I don't believe she knows. Best not to question her any more. We have four weeks until I have to go back to Europe. Perhaps they can provide the answer. Dismiss the thought of what it would mean to lose her. Right now it's important for her to know that she is free.

I say, "You are free."

° ° °

I have a dream. An airplane—an SAS DC 9—is about to land. Shortly after the landing the plane has to go through a tunnel in the side of a mountain. But as it is about to touch the ground, a horse and a carriage from the 18th century come in front of the tunnel opening. Both the horse and the carriage are a light transparent green, from quite another sphere. In order to keep from hitting the horse and carriage, the plane goes up again, but it is too late to clear the mountain. The nose of the plane collides with the wall above the tunnel opening. The undamaged plane turns around and taxis along the runway in the opposite direction. A flock of children come out of the plane. A boy runs toward me. I take him in my arms and comfort him. "I want to go traveling again," he cries.

I wake up. The first thought that goes through my mind is: You can't just knock at the door and expect it to be opened.

° ° °

One evening, Anne and I have a strange experience before the fireplace. I am sick and tired of myself, would rather discover things within her. There are no lights on in the room. Only the light of the fire casts its glow.

I enter the passage through her eyes. I forget myself, go out of myself. And I see, or sense in her, several dimensions.

I say, "You are someone from the Roman Empire."

I *see* this person. He is real. Someone from Rome, Pompeii perhaps, two thousand years ago. I see the close-cropped hair, the eyes, the cloak.

"You are a young man," I say. "The face, the slender neck, the light curly hair, belong to a man around twenty."

"Have you seen him before?"

"I haven't been aware of it. But now I see it. It is real. It is not of this life."

"And who are you?" she asks.

I know the answer: "I am all places. At all times," I say. Yes, that's the way it is. What a discovery! This is nothing strange. I only know it. I am all places, at all times.

"You have experienced a great insight," Anne says.

I gaze down along her slender, naked body. What a miracle, what an incredible revelation of beauty a human body is! God's greatest creation. But we must take care of it. What a shame to let it fall into decay! To let God's image fall into decay!

I stare at Anne's face. Then, behind the Roman—long, long before the Roman—secretively, I see the Indian woman again. She is sitting in front of me. *This is real.* This woman is real. She is sitting in front of me. I see her. The narrow nose, the dark eyes, the glistening black hair, the naked, golden brown body, the jewel, round as a little mandala, hanging down on her stomach. She arouses me, just as she did before. There is no longer any doubt in my mind. This woman exists, somewhere inside Anne or have I projected her onto her? And I can see her with my eyes open.

I am delighted, because I am also here in the room. I look around at the fireplace, the red bricks, the flames, the table with the glass figurines, the chair by the window, the yellow curtains. I am here as well. This is also real. I am so intensely *present.* So aware. I realize: Not until you really are present here, experience *this* world as real, not until then can you continue and experience other worlds equally as real. To search for other worlds because you have no roots in this one does not lead anywhere. It becomes a mist, flickering, in the clouds, an escape. It is *this* world that is real. *Now.* This is the one we are to live in. But when we are able to experience this world as *truly* real, we are also able to experience other worlds in ourselves as just as real. Because they *are* just as real. Even though I have been there so many times, I haven't really understood until now, at this very moment. But now I do. The other reality *is* real. I must take it seriously. This is a great discovery. It makes me feel that I *know*. I know that there is something more, that another reality exists, because I have experienced it myself. This is a very unique feeling, that you *know* because you have experienced it.

"I have never been so happy," I say, smiling at Anne joyously.

Suddenly I hear myself saying, "I can turn time off."

I didn't know this before. "Time is not something that can be taken for granted, the way we think," I say. "Time is something that we have created for ourselves. We have become the slaves of clocks. But time exists, if at all, only in the world of matter. In the other realm, there is no time."

I am filled with insight. "We needn't have done it like that," I say. "Why did we do it like that? We have created a limitation for ourselves."

I close my eyes. Images from the other world appear before my eyes. But everything happens in slow motion, almost without movement. There is an enormous white stairway. The broadest, most iridescent stairway that I have ever seen. It is bathed in light. A goddess descends the stairs. Yes, she must be a goddess. She is wearing a long, ethereal, shimmering gown. But she is barely moving. According to our concept of time, it would take her forever to come down. Yes, precisely, an eternity.

I say to Anne, "The tempo of our world is terrible. It is madness. It is not like this in the other world. There is hardly any tempo at all. It is as if time is standing still. If I choose I can turn it off."

Anne puts another log on the fire. Comes over and sits down close to me. I put my arm around her.

"I am alive," I say. "At this moment. I don't need a future. I don't have to possess you. Have any claims on you. To be with you *now* is enough."

"If I could come this far..." says Anne.

"As a matter of fact, I think I relish you, delight in you, *because* you are free," I say. "Perhaps we are only capable of enjoying that which is free. That we cannot enjoy and possess at the same time."

We sit staring at the flames in the fire. I feel that Anne is not here. That she is trapped in her own thoughts which she is unable to put aside.

"Switch off your brain!" I say.

"What?"

"Switch off your brain!" Now I am the therapist, and she is the client. I place my hand over her forehead and her temples. Try to help her switch off her brain.

I place my other hand on her stomach. "Breathe!" I say. "You're not breathing."

She breathes. "I have a knot in my stomach."

I hold my hand there. "Breathe into the knot."

She breathes.

"Does it help?"

"Yes."

"How does it feel to be you?" I ask.

"Good. I like being a woman. I like who I am."

"Why are you so afraid of facing things?"

"This fear wells up inside me."

"Oh?"

"I feel it now because we are talking about it."

"What does this fear look like? Try to see it."

Anne lies back with her eyes closed. "There is something black. Something big and black."

"What is it? Is it a person?"

"I am tiny, a baby, perhaps. Somebody has placed something over me. A blanket, perhaps."

"Who has placed it over you?"

"I don't know."

"Do you know why this person has placed it over you?"

"I don't know. Perhaps to make me keep quiet."

"Breathe into it. Become the little girl. Who has the blanket over her. What does she feel?"

"Perhaps they want to kill me."

"Who?"

"I don't know."

"It makes no difference," I say. "Feel the black blanket."

"Yes. It's smothering me."

"Feel it! That it is smothering you. What do you do?"

"I must get it off me!"

"Then get it off you! Throw it!"

Anne thrashes her arms. "Yes!"

"Get rid of it! Throw it off you!"

"Yes! Oh, good God!"

"How do you feel?"

She lies still. Starts to cry. "Good."

I hold her in my arms. Let her cry for a long time. "You were brave now. Is the blanket gone?"

"I think so."

° ° °

We are sitting in the living room after breakfast the next day. I am reading an article by Stanislav Grof. "Listen to this," I say. "This is what I experienced yesterday." I read to her: "Unitive consciousness can be associated with a convinced sense of gaining access to ultimate knowing and wisdom in matters of cosmic relevance.... This is usually accompanied by a feeling that such knowledge is ultimately more real and relevant than all scientific theories or perceptions and concepts of our everyday life."

Anne does not speak. She is wrapped in her own thoughts.

I still have an echo of the other "time" in me, the slow time. It feels good to slow down and just "be."

I look at Anne. "How does it feel to be rid of the black blanket?"

"Good. But there are more of them."

She looks away. If only I could help her. I think I understand what love is. It is not a question of my needs now.

I'm not going to stand in the way if she wants to be free. "Now that I know that I can turn off time, live in the present, that I don't have to own you, it might be easier."

"Living together or apart?"

"Both."

"Your wanting to possess me has been a problem for me," she says, "It feels as if you want to control me."

"I know that. I didn't know it before. Perhaps I can improve now."

Anne stands up. "I must go," she says. "I would just like to say... that I have so much to thank you for."

"And I you."

"You have taught me what patience is."

"Patience?" I exclaim in disbelief.

"What love is," she says.

I close my ears to the sounds of farewell.

Anne has gone. She has her work and her Ph.D. thesis. What am I going to do? I know one thing: I must continue on my journey. Not by plane, perhaps, but by horse and carriage from the 18th century. Strange, but at the same time as I feel that I am subject to something guiding and using me I have never before had such confidence that I am master of my own life.

If the doors of perception
were cleansed, everything will
appear to man as it is, infinite.

William Blake

When I meditate, I feel in the
thoughts and images that throng
about me, reflections of personality;
but there are also windows in the
soul, through which can be seen
images which have been created
not by human but by divine imagination.

George Russell

A week later we are having lunch at the local inn.

"I've been to see a lawyer and made arrangements for the divorce papers today," Anne says.

We had agreed. I've been expecting it. But, nevertheless... I sit there with a feeling of having been rejected.

At night I lie in bed and look at her beautiful young face, almost without a wrinkle. I say, even though I do not want to say it, "So now you'll be free to be with another man."

"Is this what you think?"

"I don't think anything. I dare say that's the way it is."

"I'm going to learn how to enter a plane without being afraid. To ride an elevator."

"And for that reason you have to be divorced from me."

Don't be bitter. Try to look at it humorously. I don't like it, but a feeling of contempt flashes through my mind.

She says, "I have to find out why I can't stay married."

I don't want to sulk, to shut her out. "Perhaps, unconsciously, you're so strongly attached to your father," I say, "that you can't commit yourself 100% to another man." I haven't forgotten the ghost I saw behind me that Sunday morning.

"I don't know. I only know that I have to find myself."

I don't stop. "You have to experience your 'programming.' Not until you experience this can you be free."

"I don't know what my 'programming' is," Anne says helplessly.

I feel a surge of tenderness. I take her in my arms.

"Forgive me for causing you so much pain," she says and starts to cry.

"The problem is that you're afraid of surrendering completely," I say.

"I've always been like that. The greater the intimacy, the more frightened I become."

"And the more panic-stricken you are to get out of the relationship?"

"You've hit the nail right on the head."

"Could there be anything forbidden or dangerous about this intimacy, when you look back upon it?"

She evades the question. "It's not that I don't love you. It's our situation that's so hopeless. I have to be here in order to work. You can't continue to commute back and forth across the Atlantic."

"I was beginning to make up my mind to move here."

She probably didn't hear what I said. "The more intimate we become, the more difficult it is. Every time—the first week after you leave—I almost go out of my mind."

Now I'm the one who feels guilty. "You needn't feel guilty," I say. I think: How despicable I've been! I've been secretly blaming her for a clarification that had to come someday, in spite of everything.

I say, "We're making this decision together. OK? It's best for both of us. It's *our* decision that we want a divorce."

Anne looks at me. "Remember, we are the school of life to each other. But why should it cause so much pain?"

"Otherwise, it probably wouldn't help," I reply.

Before we fall asleep, we snuggle up together. I love the warmth from Anne's naked body. I think I was fifteen the first time I became aware of the warmth of another person. I was in love with a girl of my own age. We had gone for a walk and stood breathlessly in front of her gate in the dark autumn evening. We kissed each other, quickly and clumsily. I felt the warmth of her body rising from under her blouse. I was timid, embarrassed, shy and confused. I had never experienced such intimacy before. When I was little, I liked to lie in the warm air behind the vacuum cleaner. There I had this good feeling of being invulnerable. This was the closest...

Anne curls herself around me even more. Like wrapping paper, I think. "This is our reward," she says, "for graduating, yet another day."

° ° °

Another week has gone by. Anne and I have gone to the mountains in Vermont in order to visit a Benedictine Monastery where I stayed for eight days two years ago. This time we spend the night at a nearby hotel.

Anne and I are proud of ourselves. We have never been such good friends. To be sure, it is easier to put up with each others' irritating habits, as long as we know that we won't have to live with them for the rest of our lives. But it is a strange feeling to live together lovingly and know that in a couple of weeks it will be over. It is difficult to comprehend that we are going to be divorced. We don't even know if it will be forever.

I notice how we are letting go of what we felt were our rights. This is good training. We talk much more openly about the life we both have apart from the other. Former objects of jealousy lost their "charge." We no longer have any claims on one another. We say: "This is the way it should always be. Not owning. Just being grateful for what we can give and receive."

I probably ought to mention that I have been having nosebleeds lately. My well-known signal that something is wrong. Several years have gone by since the last time.

Our hotel is a small castle. Built of blocks of stone, hewn out of the ground on which the hotel stands. On the inside, the floors, walls and ceilings are made of magnificent wood—carved Mexican mahogany and American oak. The fireplace in the great hall is made of French marble. Our room is as large as the sitting room of a great manor house—with a parquet floor, beams in the ceiling, French flowered wallpaper from the turn of the century, and a cozy fireplace of old red stone, framed in rough oak.

We are sitting in the library, in front of another of the hotel's twelve fireplaces. I have the feeling that I belong here, that I have been here before.

I say to Anne, "Perhaps this is where we lived when you were the Duchess. I've always thought it was in England."

"I have never lived here. It must have been in England."

We hold hands. "But you were the Duchess," I say.

"Oh, I don't know."

"Well, you weren't the maid, my dear."

We laugh. We always hold hands. Driving a car, when we go for walks, or are sitting together, as if we want to hold onto each other. People must think we're on our honeymoon, hardly our divorce trip.

"I wonder what's the meaning of it all," Anne says. "Why we came into each other's lives."

"Well, it wasn't so you could stay in the kitchen."

"I dare say there is a time for everything." Anne is serious.

"Yes, but it's difficult to turn the page," I say, "In the Book of Life."

We are sitting in the dining room, another magnificent room with wooden panels and carved doors.

Anne says, "Look around at the people eating. They remind me of the cows we drove past today. They eat and eat. Do nothing Do nothing else but eat. What is the meaning of life?"

I ponder this carefully for a long time and wonder if I can answer. At last I say, "Life."

Anne looks at me.

"The meaning of life is life. We cannot know any more."

"That was a good answer."

We are eating fish. I still have this slow tempo inside me, this feeling of everlasting peace. I say to Anne, "What can I do for you?"

"Write. Well. Then you will make me happy. What can I do for you?"

"Be yourself," I reply. "Don't become alienated to yourself."

She holds my hand even more tightly. "Thank you for understanding."

I feel that my nose is starting to bleed again. I grab my handkerchief. "Perhaps I understand too well," I laugh.

She smiles her radiant smile. When she smiles, every sorrow is erased from her face. Her smile is so sparkling. That smile could make any man's nose bleed. How will I ever manage to live without this woman!

We have come to the dessert. A young couple is sitting at the next table—a beautiful, dark-haired girl who looks Mexican, and a young man with an open, expectant face. The waitress brings in a bowl of flowers which she places in front of the girl. On the dish is a silver lid. The waitress lifts the lid. Under it is a beautiful engagement ring, with a large diamond surrounded by many small ones. The girl is speechless. The young man's eyes are shining with pride. I think: May it last for many, many years!

° ° °

We are sitting in tiny chapel of the monastery. Twelve Benedictine monks have their retreat here. They are known throughout the United States as "The Singing Monks." Their prayers and religious services include songs that they have written themselves. Three of them accompany the songs on guitars. In addition, they make wood carvings and jewelry, cultivate vegetables and trees, and, in general, take care of all the practical matters in their little society. I had stayed here as their guest.

It had been a week torn out of the calendar. Flashback: I am sitting by the window of my room. The snow is falling. At least a foot-and-a-half must have fallen since the night before. A tractor is clearing away the snow. Behind the wheel sits a man wearing yellow overalls, earguards and a helmet. It is one of the guitar-playing monks. He climbs down, finds a wrench and adjusts the angle of the snowplow. Then he climbs back into the seat, backs the tractor, and tackles the snowdrifts at full speed. A little later the monastery bells begin to chime. I go down into the chapel. The monks enter in their greyish brown cowls. The tractor driver also comes in, with his guitar under his arm. He rubs and blows on his ice-cold fingers. This struck a chord in me.

While I was growing up, I had reacted strongly against Lutheranism, the official state religion of Norway. I felt that it had rejected the mystical core of Christianity: "My kingdom is not of this earth." It had become intolerant and moralizing and gave stones for bread. I was no doubt experiencing, as Jung says, "One of the main functions of formalized religion is to protect people against a direct experience of God."

I realize now that I had thrown the baby out with the bath water. Now I was searching for the infant again.

Before I had made up my mind to go to the monastery, I had been having private conversations with another Benedictine monk, a highly gifted man with university degrees in art, anthropology and psychology. I had told him about my experiences in non-ordinary states of consciousness. He had listened with interest.

Among other things, I had confided in him about some of my experiences during hyperventilation at the Esalen Institute. One of these was very much like a near death experience: I had been breathing as deeply and rapidly as I could for an hour, when the oxygen and the music suddenly took effect. I had experienced the energy from fifteen others in the same situation in the room. When I finally let go, there was an explosion inside my head and I thought: Now I'm dying! I was bathed in a wonderful light.

A figure, I experienced it as God, had come for me. Being in this light was beyond any human experience. It was pure love.

I was not afraid, not the least bit afraid.

It was all right for me to die now. It was my turn.

I had lived my life. A good life. The time could come.

A solemn feeling came over me, and I was filled with humility and thankfulness.

I gave myself to it. I felt safe as I was being carried away. Up into the golden light.

This experience had been so intense, had so completely filled my soul that six months later, I was unable to talk about it without the tears pouring down my cheeks. Even today, as I write this, I still feel humble and grateful.

When I had this experience, I was unfamiliar with research into near-death experiences. I believe I may say that, after what happened during these moments, I am no longer afraid of dying.

The other instance that I told the monk about was this: One morning, when Anne and I had come down to the Institute from our love nest, we were informed that Richard Price, one of the leaders at Esalen, was dead.

For several days there had been a terrible downpour. A forest fire, earlier in the year, had loosened the layers of the earth on the mountainside. The rain increased the danger of a landslide. And large boulders had started rolling down the steep slopes.

Dick Price had a favorite spot up in the mountain where he usually sat and meditated. Despite the fact that he knew how dangerous it was, he had gone up there the night before. As he sat there, an enormous stone had come hurtling down and struck him in the head. He died instantly.

The day after his death, we had had a session with hyperventilation. It was my turn to breathe, and as usual, Anne was sitting beside me. When I came to the point where I let go of control, I *was* suddenly up on the mountain with Dick Price at the spot where he had been killed the night before. He sat there smiling at me.

"Don't be afraid," he said. "Just take it easy. There's nothing to worry about. Everything will be all right."

I stayed with him for a while, shared his peace. When I returned, I wondered why *I* should visit Dick Price. I hardly knew him. Had never spoken a word to him. He had lectured to us a few days before he died. Up there, on the mountain, I had experienced his friendship.

° ° °

I had said to the monk, "I feel a spiritual message in these experiences. But I don't belong to any religion. I ask myself: Who am I to think that I can stand alone, with my private God?"

The monk had looked at me contemplatively. "God's grace is not reserved for religious institutions," he had said. "It embraces everyone who is born on this earth."

"One question is important to me," I said. "Do you accept all religions as equal?"

"Absolutely." His eyes were shining. "We must stop discussing religions, and worship God together. Discussion leads us nowhere."

"I've had problems with the concept of God."

The monk smiled. "You don't have to use that word. We are in need of 'something' that knows us. And this 'something,' which we feel knows us, we call God."

"What does it mean to believe?"

The monk looked at me. "A wood carver was carving a piece of wood. A boy stood watching him. At last it became a horse. 'How could you know that the horse was in there?' the boy asked."

I had laughed.

"Grace always helps us out," said the monk. "God sends us something to make us laugh."

I looked at him, searching for an answer. "That is all very well, but what am I to *do*?"

"Build bridges." His warm, intelligent eyes sparkled. "Between your inner experiences and your creative life."

° ° °

I hope that's what this book is about.

° ° °

It feels good to sit in the simple little chapel again. There is nothing tawdry here, only rough hewn wooden constructions. The walls and ceiling are painted white between the dark brown beams. The floor is paved with natural grey and rose stones. The altar is a simple wooden table in front of several upright planks, with a crucifix the way a child would have made it.

Two years seem like a long time. I whisper to Anne, "I don't know the man who sat here two years ago."

"I don't know the woman who brought you here."

"You have been my teacher."

"And you mine."

"You have opened a new world to me."

"And you to me."

"Thank you," I whisper.

"Thank you."

We sit quietly. The chapel fills with people. Twelve monks come in, take their places. Several of them recognize me and smile and nod. It warms my heart.

I haven't been to services in any church since the last time I was here. I have problems accepting intolerance. I believe the various religions of the world are ways that human beings have found to express their innate spiritual longing, and that they have been molded by history and the location where they were needed. Also, I'm a skeptic when it comes to people who believe they have a monopoly on God, that they can tell us what this concept of God—from another dimension—says or doesn't say.

What has always impressed me about these monks is that they *live* what they teach. Here I feel my resistance to the godliness melt away. I sit and look at these twelve men.

They have chosen their lives. Here they live in brotherhood, with all kinds of practical tasks, totally devoted to their God. I look at their peaceful faces. I read serenity, friendliness and humor in them. Their humility is genuine. I recognize their simple dignity. They have come a long way. In all likelihood, the way has not been easy. They have had their trials. And the answer: "Endure it. If you stay with it, it won't stay with you." And the serenity has come in the end.

Today, the theme is "Forgiveness." How impossible it is to live without it. We must learn to forgive, in the final analysis, ourselves. One of the monks prays for all humankind, *all* people, for their right to be themselves. He mentions the rights of every religion, every race, women's rights, the rights of the homosexuals, the rights of the poor and the oppressed. And finally he prays for the Church to be renewed, to have a new heart. I think: This is what I call tolerance.

I am not very familiar with the teachings of the Catholic Church, but I think these monks must deviate considerably in doctrine.

On the way home, Anne and I talk about "grace," this moment of redemption, in which the burden of your brain—self-reproach, feelings of guilt, self-centeredness, all the barriers we place upon ourselves—disappear, and we are filled with peace. Humans have always been searching for it. This longing is the driving force behind humanity's need for nature and art, music and alcohol, worship and narcotics. Grace is God's gift of love.

We receive it, whether we deserve it or not. Must we *believe*? No, I think, not even that.

My loving you can never be an abdication of my own self. I could possibly give up my life for you out of love, but I never deny my identity as a person.

Love is a decision and commitment...

John Powell

During one inner journey I came to a place that was so alien that it couldn't possibly be on Earth. It had no landscape—with fields and trees and mountains and lakes and colors like those we are accustomed to. It was much more barren, as if everything were made of metal. It was quite "populous," but the inhabitants were not human beings. They were entirely different creatures. I saw them largely at an angle, from above, great crowds of them, thousands of tiny creatures, each with a kind of hood on its head. Here, too, were death and suffering. At first I thought there was a war going on. But it gradually seemed more like a volcanic eruption. There were flashes from powerful detonations that shed an intense red glow on the horizon of the same red color as glowing embers. Many of the creatures were suffering. A female figure, who was much bigger than the rest, was comforting them. It was as if she could embrace them all, as if she were their salvation.

Why was this shown to me? What was the meaning of it? Was I on another planet? Was it past, present or future? Was it symbolic? It seemed as if I had a choice to remain on this other planet or go back to Earth. I chose Earth. And the same thing happened as before. Everything here became so much more intense and real. I was present to an even greater extent. And I was able to distinguish, with clarity, the genuine from the false.

It is Christmas. During these last few days, Anne and I have been together twenty-four hours a day, making love, holding hands. I place her hand on her stomach and say, "Thank you for lending me your hand."

Love does not spring from everyday consciousness, it is more deeply-rooted. This is why it is so difficult for us to cope with it, to understand it. We think we can control it. We can repress it. But the great wave is there. Sooner or later it will wash against a shore in our mind.

I am sitting in our living room, gazing at the old trees and the river. I am fond of this place. Every tree is its own majesty. The winter sun makes the bare trunks look like living beings. Does the tree have consciousness? I think so. The tree is alive. Shouldn't the life and growth of a hundred years result in consciousness? Deeper and more peaceful, perhaps, than ours.

The river is calm and reflects the other bank. The meadow is still green. It is beautiful, so incredibly, boundlessly beautiful. What a planet! Now that I have been other places, my eyes have been opened. We must take care of this planet! Blasting, chopping, wasting, polluting, we behave like mad beings, consumed with greed. Instead, we should rejoice in our creations and treat them with veneration and a sense of beauty. Beauty is its own reason for being—not something devalued for a profit. Beauty is exhilarating, vital, wherever it is found, in buildings, highways, in whatever humans make. Shabby and ugly surroundings degrade us. This planet is our gift. It appears we have forgotten this.

° ° °

We are at the lawyer's to sign the papers. As the law requires, he asks, "What is the reason why this marriage doesn't work?"

Anne and I look at each other. We mumble something about it working very well. We discover that we are sitting, holding hands.

"That won't hold water in court," the lawyer says. "Do you have any children?"

"We have a monkey," I answer. We have a toy, cloth monkey named 'Apricot.' "It's going to live with me. With visiting rights for Anne."

Afterwards we go out and celebrate with an expensive dinner. We eat in silence. We are accustomed to sharing every thought. Now we sit here—each on our own island.

"Are you happy now that we are divorced?" I finally ask.

"I'm in conflict with myself."

"No you're not. Your mind is made up about this. I give you credit for that."

"We're not divorced yet," Anne says.

"Between ourselves. We've signed the papers."

"It doesn't happen so quickly."

At home in the bathtub together, we cry.

At night I am unable to sleep. I lie thinking about my life these past years. Like this book, it started as a bud. Now I have a feeling that the blossom is about to unfold.

I dismiss the thought of life without her. Just now, I am grateful for everything she has given and taught me.

Am I really so strong that she is unable to grow freely with me? Since I became aware of it that morning, I have tried to restrain myself. But, even if I would like to help her, I realize that she is the only one who can live her own process. Well, she has managed to tear herself away. When she awakens, I will congratulate her. My exceptional woman. No, no longer mine. No more ownership of "mine and thine."

I'll journey further. I know that I will never come to the end of the road, but there are still a few doors at which to knock. I don't think the Luminous Being has spoken her last.

The next morning my nose starts to bleed. I dare say, this is not meant to be easy. "Did it make you happy that I came to you last night?"

"Oh yes!"

"Next week after I've gone, I'll come to you every single night in your dreams."

"You will be welcome."

Oh, good God! Beloved, beloved Anne! How can I live without you?

Anne says, "I can't conceive of what it will be like to live without you."

"Are you going to?"

"Are you coming back?"

"You'll have to invite me, then."

"Yes. This is a new situation, isn't it?"

There is a pause. We are both thinking the same thing. In the end I say it: "Will you?"

"Invite you?"

"Yes."

"Do you want me to answer this now?"

"If you can."

"I want..." Anne hesitates, "you to feel independent of me."

So now I know. I think: I *must* try to understand. She *must* feel unfettered.

"I'm so proud of us," I say. "No bitterness. No sulking."

"No self-pity. Not a harsh word."

"Thanks to you, my darling ex-wife."

"Thanks to you."

The sun is shining on the breakfast table. Anne takes a sip of coffee. "Your coffee is much too strong!"

"Why didn't you tell that to the lawyer? Then he would have had his grounds for the divorce."

Anne plays with the sunbeams.

"I hope you finish your dissertation," I say, "and receive your Ph.D."

"I hope you finish your book." She holds out her hand. "I've loved every minute we've had together."

In four months I will receive the divorce in the mail.

"I have only one wish," I say. "That I don't freeze up, but continue to remain open."

"Once the door has been opened, it will remain open. You can transform the warm current into something greater."

"Into what?"

"Into something creative. Into God."

I say, "I think I can be parted from you now."

"And still feel secure?"

"Are you asking me or yourself?"

"Both of us."

As a memento, I have given her an old, black-lacquered, wooden box that once belonged to my mother. A bird is painted on the lid. "Whenever you feel insecure," I say, "take out the box and run your fingers over the wings of the bird. Then you will feel something strange."

She crouches down beside me, puts her arms around me. "Perhaps I am making the biggest mistake of my life."

I sit with my face buried in her hair.

"You are the best man I have ever known. It seems that, when I have everything I could desire, I have to throw it away. I remember when I was six, we had a black maid who used to take me with her to her sister's. This sister had the most beautiful doll I have ever seen. Dressed in a Christmas dress. The sister wanted to give the doll to me. But my mother had taught me not to accept anything. So I said "No," even though there was nothing in the world I wanted more than that doll in the Christmas dress."

"I don't have a Christmas dress," I say.

° ° °

I am leaving today. Tomorrow is our wedding anniversary. We give each other a present. It turns out that we have both bought a glass figurine. Both figures have two doves on them. Hers is supposed to hang down from the ceiling. Mine is sitting on a branch.

We look at the doves and at each other. The Romantics.

"I love you."

"I love you."

My suitcases are packed. We drive to the airport.

I say, "I guess there's nothing more to be said. It's beyond words." We sit silently, beyond words.

First, I have an hour's flight to New York. Then, eight hours to Oslo. It turns out that the Pan Am flight to New York is overbooked. I have a ticket but can't get on the plane. We rush over to the Piedmont Terminal. The plane is full. At American Airlines I get the last seat. But the plane is delayed. I barely reach SAS in New York. My luggage doesn't make it.

I fly and fly. Twenty times I've been back and forth across the Atlantic during the last three years. How long can I keep this up?

It's good to be sitting in the plane. Nowhere to go. Nothing to wait for, nothing to desire, nothing to want, only peace.

The Atlantic disappears below. Heading east, it becomes night long before the day is over. I always feel strangely sad on my way back to Norway. I don't feel very much at home there. During my journeys to America, Australia and the East, I have felt like a European. Never Norwegian. It dawns on me that there is no word for "gentle" in the Norwegian language.

I start talking with the man beside me, who is from Wisconsin. He asks me where I live. Out of habit, I say, "Connecticut."

I don't know where I live.

The only thing I know is that I want to be where there is room for new ideas, with freedom to break through convention.

People talk about roots. We say that we have to find our roots. I believe that our roots are inside ourselves, in the deeper layers of our own mind, our spiritual core. This is where to discover them.

We need not still our passions,
only cultivate our understandings.

William Blake

Anne, I am at the theater. Where is your hand?

Anne, I am walking down our roads. Where is your hand?

Anne, I am sitting at the breakfast table. It is overcast outside. How are the trees and the river?

Anne, I am unable to find an outlet for my thoughts. Where are yours?

Anne, it's so hard to laugh when you're not here.

Anne, the doors you opened are still standing open.

Thanks for the bathrobe you sent. I am writing in my new, blue bathrobe. It is so soft. Like you. It is like being wrapped up in you.

Anne, how do you spend your days? Is there a new man in your life?

Anne, I am playing the chants we heard at the Benedictine Monastery. Every detail of my daily life gives life to the thought of you.

The nights are long without sleep. Thanks for the pills you sent. But I don't take them. I would rather feel my feelings. Think my thoughts.

Anne, what are you doing? I close my eyes, try to reach you. But I am unable to find you.

What are we supposed to learn? Why do we always have to learn? Can't we just live a little?

Anne, don't be afraid. I am not making any claims on you. Fly!

Your hand on my skin was like the touch of a bird's wing.

I have experienced what love is. I am willing to pay the price.

I mix together all the sorrows of my life. Of many lives. When I meditate, other figures come to me. Losses I never realized I had suffered.

Anne, why? Why? This is so meaningless.

Tonight I lit a fire in the fireplace. I stare into the flames. I see the shapes of a man and a woman in there. The man is lying on top of the woman. They are consumed by the flames.

Today a friend said, "I think your hair has turned completely grey."

Anne, laugh a little more. I love to hear your laughter.

This is the right decision, you say. For both of us. I understand in my head. But my heart says, "No."

Do you remember one of the questions in your interview: "How does one explain God to a child?" The answer you received: "Just love it. And it will understand."

Tonight the dam breaks. You are on a cruise. I am unable to reach you by phone. I write to you:

"Darling, I shouldn't write. I know it only makes you unhappy. But I need you so desperately. I try to understand. I try to help by respecting our decision. But understand *me*. There is nothing I want more than to be with you.

I know that you must be free of something. But don't you understand, it isn't me. It is the shadows inside you. I am your adult life, could be your adult life, your source of growth.

Now I am sitting here among dead things. In our home by the river, everything was alive. I don't want to be alone, I want to go out and do something for people. Do you remember how we talked about helping patients who were dying of AIDS? Children with AIDS? Will you be a part of this? We who know that death is not something to fear. I must get away from here, to *your* country, where I feel free.

I have to ask: Is it really true that you don't want to see me again? This is so meaningless. Incomprehensible. I realize that you must go through a process of detachment, but do you have to sacrifice our love for that? Don't we have to take care of the gift that love is? If the reason is that you don't love me—enough—please say so. Please.

I love you... unconditionally."

I hesitate to send the letter. Forgive me for mailing it all the same.

The next day I receive a letter from you, which has crossed mine:

"When I close my eyes, I see the crystal blue of your eyes. I feel how we share the pain in our separation. All the love that we shared so joyously. Our time together has given us much more than words can express—has penetrated our entire being. So often these days, when I cry, I hear your voice in my ear: 'Don't worry darling, everything will be fine.' These words have come to mean so much to me.

"To grow through separation—to have a deeper connection. I feel this tonight. Darling, I have to find out why I must take this medicine. I know that you support it. That you love me so much.

"I have my ways of escaping from relationships when they become too intimate. The closer we came to each other, the weaker I became. I can only go *so* far in my intimacy, and then I get sick. I love you dearly. I respect you more than any man I have known. Thank you for being so patient with my maturing process. I hope I have brought more joy than pain into your life.

"I feel that this is a time of rebirth for both of us. Our love was the rarest and finest of wines. It will never be surpassed, so precious and glorious, an experience of grace as a symbol of love, to motivate, create and stimulate our future lives.

"I miss you, my darling, I miss you. It will take time to ease our suffering. Remember you are loved, dear, so easy to love.

"Enjoy every moment—for us both—let us promise each other to enjoy ourselves as much as we can.

"I love you."

° ° °

I assume that you have answered my letter.

The night is without sounds here where I live. I close my eyes. Everything I have said, my analyses and explanations, collapses inside me. What is left is a slight tone, the picture of a tiny bird that must stretch its wings and fly. It doesn't know why. I don't know why. Only God knows why.

PART II

WHO AM I?

We have no answer to the
question of what our task is,
what we ought to do on Earth.
We are living in the utmost darkness,
as far as who we are and why we are
here, and yet we know that there must
be a meaning.

Ernest Becker

Only those who come to recognize
that they have been living in
ignorance, and learn to release
themselves by discovering who
they are, experience enlightenment
as a new life, as "The Resurrection."

from *The Gnostic Gospels*

For some reason or other, the sunlight is so white in San Francisco. I wander up one street and down another, or rather, uphill and downhill. Look at the rows of two-storey houses—white, pale blue, light green, white again, peach, pink. I am happy in this city. I spend my days in the Japanese Tea Garden, the Botanical Gardens. In the park that goes down to the Pacific, and, as I have said, in the streets. I eat raw fish in the Japanese Center, burritos in the Mexican restaurant.

This is an inspiring city. New ideas, greater perspectives. There are no limits here. Fourteen days in San Francisco are like quenching one's thirst at a well.

I was haunted by the Lumious Being. The luminous path. I hadn't been able to follow her. Nevertheless, during the months after my encounters with her, I felt that she and her lumionous path were beginning to make themselves evident inside me. This was a source of joy, like a tiny brook bubbling merrily along, a bird singing in a tree one morning in spring. I felt more cheerful. Each day, it was as if I took a tiny step on the luminous path. The Being was constantly ahead of me, unattainable. But her summons had had an effect on me. These experiences from an unusual state of consciousness—these deep layers of the unconscious—had begun to penetrate my everyday conscious life. In short, I was beginning to look on the bright side of life.

I thought: If only everyone could meet a Luminous Being like this, who could lead them onto a path of light. Jung would undoubtedly have said that this figure of a woman was my *Anima*, the feminine in man, the source of his wholeness and creative development. But Anima is only a name, a theory. Most important is the experience itself: what she stands for and what she wants.

I was getting on nicely. But I won't deny that I missed Anne. To be honest, this was probably the main reason why I had gone back to the United States. We had talked on the telephone but had agreed to wait before we saw each other.

I hired a car and drove along the coast to Los Angeles to spend a day at the Esalen Institute where, at one time, I had been bewitched. I tried to be "de-bewitched." I wandered along the old paths, sat in the Big Room, and inhaled the fragrances. I even climbed the hill to Rooftop, where Anne and I had gone so many times and talked and laughed. I sat in the hot tub, gazed out over the ocean. I labored under the delusion that it worked. I drove away from there with peace in my soul. I thought: The bewitching is at an end. Thank God. The spell is broken.

In San Pedro, on my way to San Diego, I went out in a sailboat on "whale watch," out to look at the big grey whales which, at this time of year, head in pods from southern waters around Mexico, north to Alaska. These magnificent mammals are a wonderful sight. Shame to my fellow countrymen who helped kill off the blue whale—a mammal with a body temperature, circulatory system, cerebral and eye structure similiar to that of man.

The grey whales we saw were up to 46 feet long. They had different marks on their bodies—stripes and white spots—so we recognized each one when it came up to blow. We saw pods of up to nine whales. What a sight it was, when they all came up to blow at the same time before they fluked, beat the water with their mighty tails, disappearing into the depths!

On the way back to land we came across a school of dolphins that played around the boat. These humorous and friendly mammals have a larger brain than humans, though they probably use only a small part for their daily activities. People ask what they use the rest of their brain for, wonder if it is for the spiritual communion with which we human beings are still unfamiliar. They communicate with each other, emitting sounds on three different frequencies at the same time, each one at a speed ten times that of human speech. Not a bad demonstration of superior cerebral activity!

° ° °

Back in the United States I am ready to continue my exploration. I am with friends, a professor of psychology and his psychologist wife. I feel safe and can proceed with new experiments.

I don't know what to expect. I am completely open. Not wishing for anything, not expecting anything, produces the best results. On that first Sunday morning, in our home by the river, I experienced a physical birth of sorts. The spiritual birth takes place in small doses, a little at a time. But the labor pains are just as intense.

Every time one is born a little, one dies a little. A part of one's old ego has to die in order to make room for the new. Die in the sense that we give up a part of what we believe is ourself, the picture of ourself that we cling to, and that limits us.

It is obvious that I want to meet the Luminous Being again, listen to what else she has to tell me. Try, perhaps, to see if I can follow her a little further on the way. It is probably a good idea that Anne is not going to sit with me. The two of them might not get along very well.

At any rate I am prepared to accept whatever comes. I am free. I don't have to account for my journey to anyone other than myself.

I breathe rapidly and deeply. The journey begins. Always the same problem: letting go. That's it: surrender.

What we are afraid of, of course, is the fact that if we abandon control, what next? Will things emerge that I am ashamed of? That I am unwilling to face? But what then? It is all me. I live with it, inside me, all the time. No, I have to stop clinging to the edge of the pier and start to swim.

I go through various phases. First comes a terrible longing for Anne. I didn't know it was possible to long for someone in this way. I had repressed it. It penetrates into the depths of my soul and blocks everything out for a long time.

Then I am shown a chair. I know it is the electric chair. Always this symbol of Death, there is no way ahead without meeting Death. Afterwards, I experience that I am a fetus. I discover that I am lying curled up in the fetal position, I *am* the fetus, and at the same time, I am myself.

Now I am surrounded by several figures in white coats. They have come in order to do something to me. I don't know what. They lift up a lid, a white lid, is it the opening to my brain? They are working on something inside my brain. They are changing something inside me, is it the programming? I am unable to do anything, just have to let them continue. I am freezing so.

And then it happens: it is as if I have been struck by lightning, a flash of light. Right in my face. The past! Stop living in the past!

Suddenly she is there again, the Luminous Being. She is standing in front of me, smiling. "Follow me," she says, and signals with her hand.

Yes. I follow her willingly.

"You must turn off your brain," she says. "Forget that you are going to write. Surrender. Abandon your thoughts. Just come with me."

She is so happy and cheerful and playful. Yes, following her is the path of light. I *want* to follow her. Suddenly I understand: It means that I must put the past behind me. Scenes and people from my life pass in review. At full speed. Like pictures in an album, or a deck of cards, but they have frames around them. It is so easy to let them go, friends and family, I just send them away. All except two of them. Two people from my life, with whom I haven't settled accounts. One of them is a man from my job, a malicious and vindictive person who doesn't wish me well. In my everyday life, I tried to avoid becoming involved with him. When I think about him now, I can feel how negative forces in me—or are they outside of me—destructive forces try to gain the upper hand, make me rush into the hallucinations about Hell again.

Then I realize: It is my own choice whether I want to allow the destructive forces get the better of me. I can dismiss them. Choose to go the other way, the positive way. There in the depths: This is *my* choice. To send these thoughts away, not allow them to gain power over me, with all their conceptions of Hell, suffering and death. What a discovery! *This is my choice.* With my will. I have a free will. Not to be the victim of the destructive forces, to be possessed, but to be able to send them away. This is my choice. Send them away, not repress them, mind you.

The other person is Anne. The rest of the pictures disappear one by one. But Anne remains. She goes out of the frame, and takes a few steps toward me. I want to send her away as well. I want to follow the Luminous Being. I don't want to be left with anything. But I cannot get rid of Anne. Not with my will, either. She stands there. She will not go.

The Luminous Being disappears. I would like to have followed her to the Land of Bliss, a joyful place without sorrow. I had to let her go. Is it true that I mustn't be tied to anything, anyone? Be absolutely unattached? This time I was close.

I lie still, feel profoundly peaceful. My breathing is calm and regular. Then I experience something strange. It is as if I am looking inside my brain, into my system, and I see that a total change in my comprehension of reality is about to take place—a "rearrangement" of the programming. A highly unusual experience. It is not being controlled by my will, it is just happening to me. I am observing it. It is being controlled by something—on high? Outside? I don't know. Greater than "myself."

Anne is being re-programmed in me. My conception of her, my attitude to her. My feelings for her, I don't know. At any rate, I see her in a different light. I seem to have dissociated myself from her, so that I am able to regard her less emotionally and more realistically. She is becoming a part of the past, purely and simply. I am taking the first step on the path away from her. What is strange is the fact that this is also true of the first part of this book. It is something that has been, something that no longer concerns me. As if it has been written by a stranger.

This is not only a strange displacement of time. It is also a conceptual change. And I watch it taking place quietly. The figures in the white coats are gone. But I am certain that they have something to do with this. Symbolically, I assume.

Or are they to be found in a different dimension that is literally "out of this world"? That exists parallel to the everyday dimension in which we live? If *this* is the case, it may explain many things: creatures in UFO's and all the other so-called "supernatural" occurrences in the world. I don't know. I have had such experiences. I do not expect to understand them.

° ° °

It is daybreak. Everyday awareness has taken over, but the echo of the other world accompanies me. The echo gives me peace. It seems as if the reprogramming has borne fruit. I feel greatly relieved, as if I have been through a tunnel, and there was light at the other end.

As the day goes by, I experience, more and more, how the rearrangements of the night prevail. Anne slowly becomes someone else to me, changes character. I see that life with her was not only rose-colored. It was difficult. As it had to be when one does not give first priority to one's partner. One illusion after the other vanishes. I can hear her cheerful voice saying, "Hi, darling!" without feeling sad. I can see her beloved eyes before me, and wish her luck on the way to finding herself.

Life with Anne, what was it? What is truth? And what is illusion? Is it merely a question of the eyes that see?

How remarkable the human mind, the truly great mystery! I am grateful for having gained a glimmer of insight into the way it functions.

The decisive question for man is:
Is he related to something infinite
or not? That is the telling question
of his life.

C. G. Jung

I wish to continue this journey into the unknown. Perhaps what I experience will shed light on the question that has concerned man at all times: Who am I?

Not me personally, first and foremost, this is not the most interesting, but me as a representative of the phenomenon "Man," for all mankind. Who are we? What does it mean to be a human?

Are we simply material beings who function in accordance with biological laws? Or are we also spiritual beings with unlimited awareness, beyond the here and now? What do they contain—these oceans of unconscious life that we swim in and have such limited access to? We catch a glimpse of them now and then in dreams or sudden intuitive flashes. Hypnosis can open the door. Meditation may help us to keep it ajar for longer periods. But for an *exploration* of the unconscious, the most effective methods are undoubtedly of the kind I have described in this book—for Westerners at any rate. Man has been on the moon. But we know hardly anything about our inner selves. And this, of course, leads to the question of our immortality. To quote Jung: "A man should be able to say he has done his best to form a conception of life after death, or to create some image of it—even if he must confess his failure. Not to have done so is a vital loss."

But, at the same time, this means serious questioning: What do I want with my life?

What is most important to me? What is so important that it is a question of life or death? Not physical death, at first, but spiritual death. To me, the answer to this question now is to say "Yes" to my own destiny. I believe that I have freedom of choice. To say "Yes" or to shove everything ahead of me. But if I shove it ahead of me, it will still catch up with me at the next crossroads. I don't believe I can escape my destiny. I believe, more and more, that a course has been staked out, which I do not know, but which it is in my best interests to follow. Or let me call them opportunities that have been prepared for me, challenges for growth and development, which I may choose to embrace or not. If I do not seize the opportunity when it is there, it may be tougher the next time—without pity.

To me this course is symbolized by the Luminous Being. It is reasonable to ask "Why?" The answer is that I believe that experiencing her at the inner level may lead me to a greater identification with the creative forces in myself, and in life, to a greater understanding and love. To me, the Luminous Being has become the connecting link between my crystal-clear common sense and my unconscious. She has become my guide in this boundless land. I feel she can help me penetrate into a little of the secret of the personality. Not by philosophical paths, and more or less fruitless analysis, but through experience and practice which, to me, is the only viable way. How can anyone express an opinion about something he cannot know anything about because he hasn't experienced it?

° ° °

Anne and I had agreed to meet again. At first we talked about staying at a hotel for a couple of days. But at the last minute, we opted for the house by the river.

I flew to New York from San Francisco. The plane was late, and I missed my connection, spending three hours on the bus instead. At one o'clock in the morning, Anne waited for me at the bus terminal.

It had been three months since we had seen each other. But because of what happened during my last inner journey, it felt like three years. There she stood, my dearest one—but this woman was also a stranger to me. Was this the way she looked? Was it this face? So much younger than I could remember. Even more beautiful, but less mature perhaps. It was like meeting my Anne, plus or minus something. I saw things in her face, things that I had not seen before, a surprising innocence, for example. And I didn't find features that I had pictured, that I had figured to myself.

Our union was cheerful. In high spirits we drove home to the house by the river. There we sat in the kitchen, in our usual places, and talked until four o'clock in the morning. But it wasn't like two familiar old lovers. It was more like experiencing the seeds of a new relationship. Like entering a relationship with a new woman, a relationship that felt entirely different from the one we'd had before. Blind infatuation was gone. I saw us much more down to earth. I felt a kind of love one has for a friend.

I must admit that I sat and thought: Should we? Shouldn't we? With a vivid recollection of all our past difficulties—geographical distance, different cultural backgrounds, and much more—I was really in doubt as to whether we should resume our relationship. At the same time, I knew all along that we had no choice. There was still something unfinished between us, from previous lives, if one wishes to believe in that. At any rate, I felt that if we didn't find our way to completion, we would have to start all over again.

Eventually we went to bed. For a long time we lay together without touching, almost strangers to each other.

Our reunion was like experiencing love for the first time. An awareness so intense, a tenderness and sensitivity as clear as crystal. So this is what making love is. This is how eternity is contained in a moment.

We did not stay together for just two days. I remained with Anne for three weeks, until I had to go back to Norway. During this time, we began the painstaking task of building up a new and different partnership. Once again we had to accept without losing heart that Anne suffered from "commitment phobia." We knew that we had to arrange our relationship to enable us to live independent lives without possessing one another. The separation had been good for us—experiencing what it meant to give each other up completely. Now, like the oak tree and the willow, separately rooted, we could grow side by side, without overshadowing each other.

It wasn't easy, this balancing act. But again I will maintain that it was something both of us had to learn, something fate had in store for us. There was no other solution. Later we went on a vacation to Greece together to celebrate.

° ° °

My next exploration was not successful. Even before we began, I could feel the resistance inside me. I had no desire, nor was I prepared once again, to leave my comfortable, harmonious, everyday consciousness. I decided to experiment, gradually, and as the doors to my inner realm began to open, I could feel how I was resisting.

First I experienced entering a hole. But further on the cave opened up, became enormous, endless, on and on, uphill and outward, in every direction. I thought: So this is how big this realm is, infinite. Nevertheless, I didn't want to go in there. I didn't want to know.

The Luminous Being appeared and said, "Abandon yourself, now."

For a moment I felt the temptation, the bliss, of simply allowing things to take their course. But I couldn't. I said, "It won't work."

"Don't you want to know the truth?" she asked.

"The truth about what?"

"About your life."

"I know the truth about my life," I protested.

Then she said, "You know *nothing*."

° ° °

This sentence stayed with me for days and weeks afterwards: "You know nothing." Was this really true? That I knew nothing? About the truth of my life?

I hadn't been able to abandon myself. And this resulted in an emotional blockage. Why hadn't I been able to let go? Was it because I was afraid of receiving an answer to the question: Who am I? After everything I have been through, what is still so difficult, so dramatic, that I don't dare facc it? Indeed, the more I experienced this, the more I realized that the reason why we get blocked is that we dare not give in and see the truth about ourselves. There is an old saying: Hell is seeing yourself as you really are. But once you do, you are so much better off.

I have mentioned Jung, where he says that the ultimate reality is to be found at the level of the unconscious and the archetypes. Once again I was able to understand the meaning of this. Shut off from my deeper self, on the outside of a barrier, I experienced how limited this everyday consciousness is. How conventional and boring. So repetitious, with so few original thoughts. We repeat what others say and believe we have hit upon it ourselves. And we are bored while we listen to people saying things we have heard a hundred times before. "Indeed, the more the critical reason dominates, the more impoverished life becomes," Jung said. I knew that I didn't want to live this way. I had to go through the barrier, have the courage to go behind the blockage, get in touch with the images from my unconscious, find my way back to originality, my inner life. That is to say, let in the forces of yin, according to Chinese philosophy, which means accepting things as they are, going with them.

I understood that when a person merely exists, superficially, with hermetically sealed doors to his deeper self, it leads to depression, stress, aggression, nervousness. On the other hand, if we open ourselves to unconscious impulses, the radiation from within penetrates our everyday lives and makes them richer and more creative. There will be crises to go through, but they will add to one's growth unless they are repressed with pills and alcohol. In the final analysis a more whole, richer personality results.

How often we have the feeling that life is passing us by, that we can't get a grip on it, that we aren't really present. At other times, we may feel wonderful, simply "being" in the moment. We understand how true each moment is and that everything emerges from the instant. The germ of the future lies in the moment. No future exists other than this germ. Of the moment.

What is needed in order to have this calm and deep contact with ourselves? Perhaps we can say: "Being the master of our own house, not getting caught up in, or driven by unconscious complexes and obsessions, not being victimized by our "programming." We *can* uncover the "programming" and then we can do something about it. We do not have to let unconscious material control us completely.

The Benedictine monk and I talked about the concept of "sin." He said, "Let us forget the word sin. It has no meaning for people today. Let's call it alienation instead. To be alienated from ourselves."

This is a language I understand. It is important that we are able to find a fragment of an answer to the question: "Who am I?"

Many transpersonal experiences involve events from the microcosm and the macrocosm—realms that cannot be directly reached by human senses—or from periods that historically precede the origin of the solar system, of planet Earth, of living organisms, of the nervous system and of Homo Sapiens. These experiences clearly suggest that, in a yet unexplained way, each of us contains the information about the entire universe or all of existence, has potential experiential access to all of its parts, and in a sense IS the whole cosmic network as much as he or she is just an infinitesimal part of it, a separate and insignificant biological entity.

Stanislav Grof

The eternal subject is this: "Has everything that has happened to me in life been coincidences? Coincidences which I have acted on—or have not acted on? Or is there a greater, invisible pattern that governs everything? Do I have a free will in order to make decisions? Or do I act in accordance with this pattern? Is it my unconscious self, perhaps, that decides, plans and sees to it that I find myself at this particular place at this particular time, where something happens to me? An unconscious part of me, about which my conscious ego knows very little, but which is a much greater part of me than my everyday mind.

Is it maybe so that my "total self" has free will, while that of my "conscious ego" is limited? It is an incredible feeling when, in a non-ordinary state of consciousness, you experience the imperative authority of your "total self" taking you by the nape of the neck. You simply must obey. You realize that the scope of your conscious ego is not as great as you thought it was. Your "total self" is the true architect of your life. Or, in the words of Joseph Campbell, "Your whole life is a plot. Who composed this plot? An aspect of yourself of which your conscious ego is unaware. The whole thing comes together like one big symphony."

Jung had *his* opinion: "The future has been prepared in our unconscious a long time in advance."

° ° °

"You know nothing," the Luminous Being had said. Is it true, that I don't know anything—about myself, about my life?

I am again with Anne in the house by the river. I ask her to help me get through the blockage I experienced the last time. She is intensely interested. She has completed her thesis and is now waiting for it to be approved. She is eager to take part in my investigative journey.

Again we are lying beside each other, on our backs. We hold each other's hand. I have a feeling that this is going to be a decisive passage.

The journey begins. I experience our arms, linked together by clasped hands, as an umbilical cord. I experience this literally. Rebirth again. And I know that the umbilical cord must be cut for the child to be delivered, grow and become independent.

I also know that I am supposed to close my eyes and go into myself. But I can't stop looking at Anne's face, the clean, classic features. And then it happens again, right before my eyes: her features change. Unbelievable. But it *happens*. It is happening to *me*. I see an Egyptian woman. Anne herself has experienced a life in Egypt thousands of years ago.

Now I see her as a priestess. It is Anne. But at the same time it is no longer Anne. Another young, dark-skinned woman. The features, the nose, eyes, mouth, make-up, and hair, the ankle-length gown of gold and jade.

We stare at each other. A violent passion is kindled in us both. We make love with an intensity that is the primal force itself between man and woman, the creative image, the sexual union of the entire human race.

Afterwards, we lie on our backs, breathing deeply and resting. I am filled with gratitude at this total abandon, having made love with an Egyptian priestess.

I look over at Anne. I see that something is upsetting her. This is not the usual, gentle Anne. Her face is closed. There is a coldness emanating from her. I ask, "What is it?"

Anne looks away. "Nothing."

Yes, there is something. I feel the door close. I hold out my hand, but she doesn't notice it. The door is closed. Am I the one she is rejecting?

I lie watching her, sympathizing with her. "Everything is all right," I say cautiously.

I catch her eye. And I see, in the depths of her eyes behind the facade, a lonely soul withdrawn from the world, withdrawn from itself.

Even though I was the one who was supposed to be travelling, it is now more important to help her. I try to hold her gaze. I want so much to reach her. She still seems to be giving me the cold shoulder. Then I hear myself saying, "The door only has a handle on the inside."

Something happens to her. She looks at me. She stares at me. I see that she understands. She experiences her own withdrawal, so unlike the woman who is smiling on the outside. I see that she is gaining insight. Cautiously, I reach out my hand and touch her face. It opens up.

She throws her arms around me and starts to cry. Sobbing bitterly. "It's my mother who is in there," she says. "I didn't know. She died when I was twelve. I don't think I ever allowed myself to grieve."

I hold her in my arms, stroke her hair and cheeks.

"I never would have believed this," she continues. "It was because I gave myself so totally, and you knocked at the door. Oh God! It has been closed for so many years."

She cries. I kiss away the tears.

"It's so unfair," she says. "I never thought I'd use that word. But that is what I felt when I lost her. This is what I feel when I can't keep you."

I don't know what to say. I lie there and experience that she is gaining awareness. If only it will help her.

"What shall I do?" she says.

I know what she is thinking. In a way, I am inside her. I see it clearly now. "You have been like this all your life," I say. "You want to leave the one you love. This struggle has been going on inside you with all your partners. It has never given you peace."

"You are quite right," she says. "But I don't want to be like this."

"Then to see it, accept it, is probably the first step."

"Perhaps I simply have to accept the fact that I must remain alone. I can't go on doing this to people."

"Grappling with doubt," I say, "is probably your process." I don't know what else to say.

There is a pause. "Now you must enter yourself," she says.

"If I can only let go."

"It is paradoxical," she says. "We need control in order to cope with life. And, at the same time, it strangles life."

"That is what the evolutionary process of an artist is about," I say, "to relax control."

I close my eyes. Open them again.

"Go into yourself now!" she says. "I want to know what's in there."

I hesitate. I am apprehensive today.

"I'll be here when you come back," she smiles.

I close my eyes again. Now I leave Anne. I am in a burial vault. There is a black coffin in front of me. Everything is black. I am in the coffin. But I am also standing on the outside, looking at the coffin. It starts to grow. Higher and higher. Turns into a tower. A black tower. The top disappears up in the sky, higher than I can see.

Then I struggle with the invisible. Something tears and pulls at my body. I groan. Anne says, "Breathe into it." I breathe. Into it. Through it. A moment of delivery. A moment of peace.

But the invisible forces threaten me again. The dog that belongs to Anne's daughter comes into the room. It sniffs at me and whimpers a little. I am happy.

"A human sound!" I exclaim. I probably meant 'earthly.' I throw my arms around the dog's neck.

Then everything crowds in on me. I see all my frailties, experience my shortcomings, everything I have failed in life. I am the most wretched. The pictures rush past. No, not past, they build up in my head, they grow and grow, becoming impenetrable. I am crushed. I cannot stand it. Why am I doing this to myself?

I lose faith in myself, in my process, in everything I do, everything I believe in. I feel that I am disintegrating, being obliterated, annihilated, destroyed. I am nothing. I groan: "I don't want this. I renounce everything. Life. Myself. If only I can be spared this."

I hear Anne whispering in my ear: "You're not a coward, are you?"

Yes, I am a coward. I give up. Then the Luminous Being is standing there. "Come," she says gently. So gently. Yes, I come. I come. I yield, a little. Bit by bit. I come! Into—LIGHT! Shining white LIGHT!

Silence. Complete silence. Blue silence. Infinitely. Blue infinity. I am floating, a speck of dust in the Universe. I have always been floating here. From the dawn of time. It is safe. I am no body. I simply am. Yes, what am I? I am a cell. A single cell. I am the cell itself. The cell is alive. I am the living cell. Never have I experienced anything so strange. I understand the life of a cell. I open myself. Absorb. Transform. Open myself. Give out. This is the life of the cell. It is life.

Strange I understand life.

I ask: "What is the secret of life?"

It answers: "Life."

I ask: "What governs life?"

It answers: "Life."

I ask: "What is beyond life?"

The answer is: "Life."

I ask: "What is the mystery of life?"

It answers: "Life."

° ° °

I transform myself into a sprout, a tiny sprout that comes up out of the earth. A mischievous shoot, in high spirits. Dancing, the Dance of Life, I am the sprout. I am conscious. The sprout is conscious.

Time is suspended. I am filled with joy. Again something strange happens. I become a tree. A five-hundred-year-old oak tree, with a thousand roots and a thousand branches. I am this tree. I am also the sap that rises *in* the tree. I breathe. With every breath I take the sap rises. Up through the trunk, out through the branches. I am the life of the tree. I am alive! Good God, I am alive!

I feel this life. Forget I ever thought of taking my own life, now I want to live! Live!

After these incredible revelations, I lie resting. After a while Anne goes down to the kitchen to find something to eat. She probably feels that she can safely leave me to my peace.

Then I have a strange vision: I am in a place that resembles a cafe. A figure is leaning on the counter over in the corner. Is it me, or another man who is there? Then I see that the head is a skull.

Death is paying a visit. My old friend Death. He wants me to accompany him again. He takes hold of me. Then I understand that, in reality, he has been there for a long time, for many years during my process of aging. I experience how each of my organs, my muscles, has aged. How they have stored up "aging." And now—I experience that I am able to prolong life. I battle with Death for muscle after muscle, organ after organ. Get rid of the stored-up aging. It is painful. But I do it! Gradually I experience renewal, that I am renewing my contract with life in every part of my body.

I must have groaned because Anne comes running. "What's the matter?" she says.

"Relax," I say. "It was only Death paying me a visit. I sent him away."

Anne looks at me thoughtfully. "What does Death look like?" she asks.

What does Death look like? The question sends me far away, through my inner landscape and out into the cosmos.

What does Death look like? Suddenly I hear myself saying, "Death looks like... sexual energy."

"Tell me more," Anne says expectantly, "if you can."

"Death is not annihilation. You understand? It is rejuvenation!"

"Does this have to do with sex?"

"*That* is what I saw. Death is a life-giving force. It is the beginning of life. Not the end."

"Death is a life-giving force?"

"The primeval force that renews life. This is what Death looks like. It is the vital force. To be born. To be free."

Anne thinks this over. "So Death is not loss of life?"

"It is the giver of life."

"Perhaps you are right. If it means being born to a new state of awareness."

"Death is necessary for all renewal. But you have to experience it yourself. Otherwise it's just window-dressing."

° ° °

The journey is not yet over. I close my eyes. I am in Africa. I am a young black chieftain. I am sitting with my wife, a young black woman. We are naked in the sun. Children are playing around us. They are shouting joyously. The woman and I are also laughing and happy. Her skin is shiny and beautiful. She is sitting with her legs apart. I place my hand on her coal-black curly hair. My love knows no bounds. My love knows no bounds.

The sand around us is reddish-yellow. The huts are orange. I have experienced being in Africa before during a non-ordinary state of consciousness. But I have never been there in this life. Have I been black in a previous life? No wonder I have always thought that young black women are beautiful.

Night has fallen. The woman and I are lying in the hut in the dark. We play tenderly with each other. I am happy. Life is good. I am the king and the lover.

° ° °

I enter the deep, silent, peaceful void again. The Luminous Being is with me. Five judges dressed in black enter from the left. In single file they go up onto the podium. With a wave of the hand I make them disappear down through the floor. I know what this means: That I must not be so self-righteous and critical.

Yet another experience is lifelike and real. I am on a farm. These are primitive times, several hundred years ago. A life of plenty. Pigs run about in the open. We laugh and drink and eat.

I open my eyes and say to Anne, " *What* these pictures are isn't always so interesting. *That* they exist at all is the important thing—and in such overwhelming numbers."

"I understand," Anne says.

"You know," I continue, "it's stupid to try to explain the mysteries. As if they were no mysteries."

"That's true."

"I wanted so much to meet the Luminous Being," I say, "but, you see, the Luminous Being is in my everyday life. I experience her every single day. I *have* met her. And she *has* flowed through me. I follow her. And that's that. I believe we must accept this limitation as human beings. To live with the mystery, in touch with the mystery, is the only thing we can do. Everything that is life will emanate from the mystery within us, an emanation from within, out to our surroundings. It is the emanation itself that counts, not the map of what is in there. Be open to the radiation."

"What is radiation?" asks Anne.

"I don't know," I answer. "What are the sunbeams?"

"Love, perhaps," says Anne.

I lie there, aware of the moment, of how valuable each moment is. It is true that pure consciousness is empty, without content. And at the same time, totally aware, lacking nothing. We need this emptiness in order to "be" in the moment.

° ° °

What became of the blockage? The purpose of this journey. I suddenly understand: it was an illusion. The blockage was an illusion. Something I created myself.

Why do we create illusions like these? We make up things in our minds. We believe they are real. Then we change our mental state, and they are gone. What were they, other than illusions?

I lie here, wondering. Why do we need these illusions? Why can't we just live with things as they are? I know it is easy to find psychological answers to this question. But I am not content to let psychology answer it. I am not buying any ready-made answers here. I want to get behind it, deeper.

The answer suddenly occurs to me: Perhaps it is because consciousness in itself is an illusion. Is consciousness illusory? That is to say, the content of consciousness. An illusion that is playing a game with us? What is it, this consciousness that we carry around? We take it for granted, but what is it? Can we be certain that all this hustle and bustle isn't an illusion?

If so, who staged the game?

Humankind knows that it cannot answer these questions. Is this why we believe that we have invented God? This is the human vantage point—because humans are unable to conceive of anything greater than themselves, or greater than humanity itself can conceive of. It may very well be that it looks quite different from God's point of view.

If the content of consciousness is an illusion, then it's true what the Luminous Being said: "You know nothing about the truth of your life." This is the answer I didn't know.

How can I know anything about an illusion? How do we see behind an illusion? And why take it all so seriously, if everything is an illusion?

° ° °

The next day I go out and say "Hello" to the old oak tree. I place my cheek against the trunk, inhale its fragrance and give it a hug.

Life is breathing in and out.
God breathed His life into man.

David Steindl-Rast

Everything that lives is holy.

William Blake

I have been to a funeral. One of my friends has passed away. I sat listening to all the words the minister said to comfort the bereaved. I thought: Why doesn't he just say that my friend is alive. I sat there, knowing that my friend's consciousness, the glint in his eye, is alive. Death is no catastrophe. I sat in the crematorium, lighthearted, thinking of my friend now happy in a kingdom of higher consciousness. I believe he was ready.

° ° °

In the park below my house an old man is sitting on a bench. He sits there every day. He has been sitting there for as long as I have been living here.

He sits with his head drooping forward, his hair long and grey at the neck. His eyes are closed. I can see his mouth. His lips are moving, but not a sound can be heard.

I sit down on the bench opposite him. I close my eyes. Tune in on the old man. At first there is silence. Then—gradually—I begin to pick up fragments of a conversation.

The old man is carrying on a dialogue with someone. I listen. His inner voice is steady and clear, not at all the voice of an old man.

"The fact is," he says, "it took me sixty years to come out of myself and really *see*... others. To care about them, for their sakes, not for mine."

"Sixty years well spent," another voice answers.

"And yet it took twenty years before I understood the secret."

"Good for you!" the other voice says.

"It is... I must believe that what I do is right. No matter what, it has a greater meaning."

It is silent for a while inside the old man.

"I've had to embellish it, you know," he says.

"What?"

"Your Creation. I've had to cover up the defects and embellish it."

The Voice laughs. "Then you were a part of the Creation."

"I was a tailor," the old man says.

Another silence.

"So that was your life," the old man says to himself. "A tiny cog in a big wheel... There is one more secret," he says, addressing the Voice.

"Well?"

"That we are not alone. We belong together—all of us—on this earth."

"You have understood so much of the Creation," the Voice says, "that I don't know if I need to send you back."

"I don't mind coming back. I'm proud of having a hand in the Creation."

"Some people believe the Creation exists for them to exploit for personal gain," the Voice says. "Others consummate it."

"But those who exploit it, aren't they also a part of the Creation?"

"Yes."

The old man sits and thinks. "I don't understand, but I accept it."

"You will understand." The Voice is warm without limits. "What has been created is free to live its own life."

"Does life have a meaning?" the old man asks. His voice is humble.

"That is the final secret."

"I have had a good life," the old man says. "Thank you for my life."

"You were lonely and unhappy."

"I cried. Because I was yearning. I didn't know for what."

"You never betrayed your yearning."

"I wept. In wonder. I saw... the clouds are colored red by the sunset. The swallows soaring in the sky."

"You made use of the gift you received—to see."

"Yes. I saw... the Creation."

There is a long silence. I open my eyes and look at the man. A few yellow maple leaves have fallen on his coat. His lips appear to be moving again. I close my eyes.

"To begin with, I was afraid. I encountered Death when I was thirteen. A war was going on. A plane crashed where I was standing. Exploded. Many dead bodies lay scattered about. I remember thinking: Moments ago, these people were sitting in the plane, talking to each other, looking out of the window, waiting to land. Now they lie here, torn to pieces. Can life be extinguished so easily, so abruptly? This thought has never left me. And Death has continued to cross my path."

Silence again. Then the old man says, "I didn't understand anything. Who was I? Only a tailor."

"You understood more with your heart," the Voice is back, "than many people do with their heads."

"Today, I am no longer afraid. No, not afraid. I am ready."

There is a crack in the clouds. A low autumn sun shines on the man, a golden light on the yellow leaves.

"You see," the old man smiles to himself, "it took many years before I was willing to admit to myself that I believed in You."

"Time," says the Voice, "does not apply to me."

"I had to get beyond all of those who told about You. They made it so difficult. But one day I understood: You just are. You are You!"

"And you are you," the Voice laughs. "What is the difference?"

"No," the old man says happily. "What is the difference?"

"Then come with me," the Voice says.

"Where are you taking me?"

"Home. Where you came from. Where you always shall return."

"Unconditionally?"

"Unconditionally."

"Have I been accepted?"

"You have been accepted."

"Just as I am?"

"Just as you are."

They are quiet for a moment. Then the old man exclaims: "I see You! I have arrived! Oh, thank goodness!"

There is a silence. I wait. Stand up and go over to the man. Then I see that he is dead.

Seeking inspiration from the Muse of Death is an old habit of reflective people.

Research on death, and dying, raises basic questions about life, and what it means to be a human being.

Death... would appear to lie on the other side, an impassable frontier. Yet there may be a method of exploring the fringes of this frontier. It is to treat the illusive "something" we call Death as if it were a peculiar state of consciousness...

The hypothesis underlying this method is that the inner side of death is, under special conditions, open to human experience before bodily death. Features of near-death experience may be observed in many unusual states of consciousness.

If we hope to make dying a more conscious process, we must begin by making living more conscious.

Michael Grosso

In the first part of this book I mentioned Near-Death Experiences (NDE). In this chapter, I refer to the work of others in this field and concentrate on the eternal questions: Is there a life after death? Do we all carry God inside us? Who am I?

According to the great Meister Eckhart from the Middle Ages, "No one can know God who has not first known himself. Go to the depths of the soul, the secret place... to the roots, to the heights; for all that God can do is focused there."

St. Augustine said, "In the depths of my heart, God is closer to me than I am to myself."

Philosopher Michael Grosso of Jersey City State College and John F. Kennedy University has written a brilliant book, *The Final Choice* (which is supposed to be on Gorbachev's reading list). With a basis in philosophy, religion, thanatology (teachings about death), history, psychology and parapsychology, he discusses the forces of life and death in both a logical and a visionary manner. He presents man's spiritual potential as the alternative to nuclear destruction.

Grosso regards the near-death experience as an archetype. "Archetype" is one of Jung's concepts, defined as a psychic dynamism that cannot be traced to the personal history of the subject. The fact that the near-death experience is regarded as an archetype means that the many accounts of NDE have features in common, independent of age, sex, education, religion or culture. People speak of their encounters with other worlds as bathed in awe-inspiring light, of beings in the form of light, and messengers from these other worlds. It is important that objects, creatures and shapes are experienced as being more realistic, more alive than in the ordinary reality.

Grosso believes that the recognition of this kind of archetype is of the greatest significance to psychology. He writes: "As Jung knew from clinical experience, 'modern man'—solitary, anxious, driven, traditionless and spiritually uprooted—has lost touch with the healing symbols and energies of the deep psyche, especially the healing symbols and energies for coping with death. The NDE is a windfall clue to rediscovering the healing force within, the living answer in our own psyches to the riddle of death."

It happens very often that people who have near-death experiences are disappointed to return. It appears as if people on the threshold of death catch a glimpse of something that lures them away from life itself.

Grosso asks: "What could it be that reverses the instinct for self-preservation? So much anxiety is spent in the course of life struggling to fend off death, yet at the verge of death, the struggle sometimes mysteriously subsides, anxiety vanishes and life in the body becomes a reason for regret. That which we cling to grimly all our lives, now we are all at once ready to discard."

I mentioned before that most people who have had near-death experiences feel that the fundamental aspect of the universe is love—unconditional love, forgiving, all-embracing, unearthly, perfect, transpersonal love. Grosso writes: "On the threshold of death, the innocent ego may, for the first time, come face to face with its unknown Self."

Jung defines this Self as: "The totality of the personality, a quantity that is superordinate to the conscious ego." And: "The Self is not only the center, but also the whole circumference which embraces both consciousness and unconscious; it is the center of this totality, just as the ego is the center of the conscious mind." And: "The Self is our life's goal, for it is the completest expression of that fateful combination we call individuality."

As Grosso expresses it: "The Self is possessed of greater powers than the conscious ego is normally aware of."

In his book, *Life at Death*, Professor Kenneth Ring, one of the leading researchers of near-death experiences, suggests that The Voice, The Being of Light and other phenomena experienced in the near-death state are the larger pattern of oneself: "It is not merely a projection of one's personality, however, but one's *total Self* or what in some traditions is called the *higher Self*. In this view, the individual personality is but a split-off fragment of the total Self with which it is reunited at the point of death."

People experience the Being of Light as divine. Many believe it is God. This was the way I experienced it during hyperventilation at Esalen—what I told the Benedictine monk.

Grosso comments on the experiencing of God in a religio-historical connection: "In the Western tradition, to claim identity of Self (however higher) with God is blasphemous. But perhaps in light of what we are learning about the near-death experience, and what is latent in the collective human psyche, we can understand how certain individuals might be led to identify with God. Jesus was accused of blasphemy because he claimed a special intimacy with the Father (John 10:33). The Hindu doctrine of the oneness of *Atman* and *Brahman* is not shy about asserting this lofty equation."

Indeed, in the Upanishads, the last part of the Vedic hymns which contains the essence of Hinduism's spiritual message, it says that Atman and Brahman are identical.

Grosso continues: "The Gnostic and enthusiastic traditions of Christianity, the *Sufis* and *Cabalists* of the Islamic and Judaic traditions all drew their inspiration, often at great risk, from the well of this Supreme Identity."

People have undoubtedly had near-death experiences at all times. Grosso believes that the mere existence of NDE makes it unavoidable for an identification with God to arise in the history of mankind. History and the History of Religion are filled with people who have had "revelations," which form the basis for our culture and religions. Examples are everywhere, from Paul's experiences on the road to Damascus to Martin Luther King.

Grosso writes: "One can also see how such archetypal experiences would, in some hardy spirits who trusted their own instincts above tradition, the kernel of a new authority, a new interpretation of reality and a new myth of personal identity."

But Grosso points out that history is also filled with examples of fanatics who have brought about disasters for themselves and others. There is no doubt that encounters with archetypes may have a malicious side. In someone who does not have a genuine spiritual life and is driven by envy, intolerance and narrow-mindedness, these energies—intended for spiritual renewal—may have the opposite effect.

Historically, feelings of absolute, inner urgency coupled with ignorance and singlemindedness, have led to wars and oppression. There are many examples, from the Christian Crusades to the Moslem Ayatollahs.

Grosso writes: "Perhaps the study of archetypal psychodynamics could help reduce these misunderstandings and show that behind the many masks of the gods is the one eternal Self in transformation."

We are back where we started. What is this "one eternal Self in transformation?" The Higher Self. To people who have had near-death experiences, and others who, in various ways, have come in contact with this Higher Self, this feeling of solemnity, of having been in the presence of a greater—call it Divine—dimension will remain with them for the rest of their lives.

This Higher Self truly has inherent powers. It leads us out of confinement, out of darkness into light. From ignorance to insight. From coldness to love. It solves the riddle of existence, stimulates self-knowledge, asks for humility in the face of the mysteries, establishes the connection between the past, the present and the future, shows the way to self-development. It is not surprising that it is interpreted by many people as "The God Within."

Jung himself had a significant near-death experience in connection with a heart attack, which he describes in *Memories, Dreams, Reflections*. In leaving the Earth, looking down, he could see from the Himalayas and the Indian Ocean to the Mediterranean. He later estimated that the distance to Earth had been 930 miles. He had the feeling that "everything was being sloughed away. Everything I aimed at or wished for or thought, the whole phantasmagoria of earthly existence, fell away or was stripped from me—an extremely painful process." He was standing on the threshold of a temple carved out of a block of stone, floating in the universe. He knew that when he stepped inside, he would meet all the people he belonged to in reality. There, at last, he would understand the historical nexus to which he or his life belonged. He would know what had been before him, why he had come into being and where his life was flowing. He would learn why everything had been like this and not otherwise.

Before he stepped into the temple, however, he experienced being brought back to Earth by his doctor, who, in the vision, appeared in his primeval form of a king. Jung was greatly disappointed. It took three weeks before he could make up his mind to live again. He regretted having to return to the "box-system," as he called it, with each person sitting alone in a box, in an artificial three-dimensional world.

For weeks during the daytime, he was greatly depressed because he had to live in this world of grey boxes. But at night, the door to his soul stood open to the most wonderful pictures: "Toward evening I would fall asleep, and my sleep would last until about midnight. Then I would come to myself and lie awake for about an hour, but in an utterly transformed state. It was as if I were in an ecstasy, I felt as though I were floating in space, as though I were safe in the womb of the universe—in a tremendous void, but filled with the highest possible feeling of happiness. 'This is eternal bliss,' I thought. 'This cannot be described; it is far too wonderful!'"

He tells of the most incredible experiences. Now he sees the nurse as an old Jewess who is preparing ritual kosher dishes, and now with a blue halo around her head. He experiences mystical, ritual marriage ceremonies from religious history. His inner kingdom consists of intense sensations of beauty, of many dimensions, in a state beyond time. Everything that happens throughout the ages was summed up in an objective whole.

He describes the way he felt about the earthly world:

"I was tormented and on edge; everything irritated me; everything was too material, too crude and clumsy, terribly limited both spatially and spiritually. It was all an imprisonment, for reasons impossible to divine, and yet it had a kind of hypnotic power, a cogency, as if it were reality itself, for all that I had clearly perceived its emptiness. Although my belief in the world returned to me, I have never since entirely freed myself of the impression that this life is a segment of existence which is enacted in a three-dimensional, box-like universe especially set up for it."

I would assume that most people who have experienced unusual states of consciousness, whether through a near-death experience, hyperventilation, deep meditation or psychedelics, agree with Jung.

° ° °

What conclusions may be drawn from near-death and similar experiences as far as the belief in a life after this is concerned? One thing is certain: people who have had these experiences are convinced that something more exists, something greater than life on earth. They no longer regard themselves in isolation. We may not have *proof* of eternal life in a tangible sense of the word. Because the other world is not "tangible."

Wouldn't it be sad... if
love should only be a
curse, because its demands alone
could make it clear, that none of us
was worth loving, instead of
love being recognizable by
the very fact that it is loving enough
to be able to find something loveable
in all of us, thus, loving enough
to be able to love us all.

Søren Kierkegaard

We humans are yearning. It may be for love, or a partner to share our life with. Or it may be for security. Often we do not know what we are yearning for. We are only yearning. Perhaps we can identify this yearning. Perhaps it is a yearning for "ourselves." For contact with our own unconscious, with our Higher Self, our independent, spiritual "I."

° ° °

Anne and I go on another journey. I am traveling. She is lying beside me. Keeping an eye on me.

Out of my everyday consciousness, I come to a totally unfamiliar place. Here are gigantic, humanlike creatures, three or four times larger than us. They have strange vehicles, white with enormous wheels, like a kind of bicycle. The landscape is intensely luxuriant and green.

My senses have now become quite open to an awareness and susceptibility that I have never known in my daily existence. They register the most imperceptible things, hear sounds that I otherwise do not hear or notice, feel the slightest touch with an intense amplification. I am lying with my eyes closed, but I can still "see" Anne beside me. I feel the energy and vibrations emanating from her, even though she is lying two feet away. And as I experience this, I feel that I am one with her. I *become* her, just as I experience that she becomes me.

I think: This fusion of two people, is this what love is? Later, when the physical separation is a fact, the vestiges of this interdependence remain. We feel both the fusion and the separation at the same time. So it is probably up to us whether this is to be experienced as happiness or torment.

I reach my arm out to Anne. She puts her arm around me. But as she does this, I feel a slight push from her arm, barely noticeable. She put her arm around me, but at the same time, she pushed me quite lightly, but firmly, away. I wonder if she noticed it. I change my position and try again.

Again the good arm, and then the slight push. It pushes me away, keeps me at a distance. It is as if it is saying: "Don't come too close. Don't be too intimate."

I try again. The same thing happens. It is obvious that she is unaware of it. It seems to be a reflex, something which is controlled from the level of her unconscious.

I ask myself: Is this something that has been going on all the time? As long as we have known each other? During all of our intimate moments? Only that at the everyday level I haven't noticed it.

But if this has been taking place, unconsciously on her part, this constant reservation, then I have probably noticed it all the same, if not consciously, then in *my* unconscious. And not only noticed it, but reacted to it some way or other. Yes, I recognize this feeling of tension, as opposed to relaxation, and this indefinable feeling of "loss." Insecurity.

I lie still and wonder about this. I feel a pain down in the small of my back. I concentrate on the pain. And suddenly I experience that I am a little child. I am lying in my mother's bed. I feel the push. My mother is giving me a slight push. My mother is rejecting me. I feel how the pain originates in the small of my back. I think: Aha! So *this* is where the first frustration settles. I thought it was in my neck, my jaw and throat. No, it is down there, inside my body somehow.

It is a sexual frustration, but it is much more. I feel that my life force and my self-expression are being frustrated.

I am the little child, and feel like one. But at the same time, I am "me," the one who is observing the child. Now I am lying here, and experience being rejected. I am "me," and experience rejection by Anne. Because I mentioned the slight push, she has turned her back on me. I am the child, and experience the rejection by my mother. This is painful. Terribly painful. I feel that I am being rejected, but I don't understand why. The only thing I feel is helplessness. My mother doesn't want me. My back hurts, I am not good enough. I am inadequate.

I lie here and feel this pain. In some sense it is located in the small of my back. But at the same time it is nowhere. It is only a feeling. The back is only a place where the feeling settles. I think: But I don't need this feeling! It is no longer real. Endure it! Endure it! Just *stay* in it, then you will get rid of it. Pictures of a little child, clenching its teeth to keep from crying, come crowding in.

I have a deep insight: "I am totally alone on this earth."

This knowledge gives me peace: "I am alone on this earth." Now that I know this, I shall be able to adapt myself to it. I didn't know this before, or rather, I didn't want to face it. I have tried to pretend to myself that I was not alone. This has been a delusion. It has been painful. Now that I have realized that I am alone, I am able to live with it.

An hour goes by. Anne is still distant. It is difficult, but I know that I have to endure this, not run away from it. And gradually, as the minutes pass, I feel that I am growing. I am growing out of it, into a feeling of independence and self-containment. A sensation of freedom that feels good. I think about my mother. Perhaps she wasn't capable of more intimacy. Perhaps she was afraid of her feelings for me. So that she had to keep them in check with that slight push. Or maybe she was afraid of stimulating feelings in me. At any rate, she didn't know any better. She did what she could and I forgive her. She was so shy.

And I think of Anne. Is this a part of her programming, perhaps? And if it is, where does it come from? I can only guess. She has to find this out for herself. It is possible that she is also angry with me. She may have her reasons for it. I thought she had gotten over it. It seems like it on the surface. But perhaps, in her unconscious, she still hasn't forgiven me.

Finding the root of these reflex actions, these impulses, is detective work. But I realize now that they are there, and have this effect without one being aware of it.

° ° °

On the following day Anne and I talk about the phenomenon of rejection, the way a little child who has been rejected—as I experienced it on the previous day—may develop, as a fundamental feature of its personality, an unconscious feeling that it *will* be rejected. To be sure, this may also have perinatal and transpersonal roots—be experiences from previous lives.

A deeply seated feeling like this molds the personality, forms the basis of attitudes. As an adult, the person may see rejection where it does not exist and will not be able to cope with the rejection in an adult manner when he does experience it. Such a person will unconsciously carry in him an exaggerated fear of "loss." In turn, this will result in a need to possess both people and things. In reality, it is a question of self-confidence, overcompensating, trying too hard, too hard in every relationship, which rarely leads to success. Then anxiety and stress arise.

I went through a hard round yesterday. I experienced rejection at a deep level, a level that is usually unconscious. But now it feels as if I have gotten rid of the rejection I may have carried with me throughout my life. And I am convinced that in the future this feeling will grow stronger. I thank Anne for her help.

The elimination of such an underlying feeling of having been rejected, or the anticipation of it, results in a totally different confidence. Nor will one experience *being* rejected so easily, because one does not invite it upon oneself.

° ° °

The next morning we wake up to a cloudless sky. I have slept so well. I am bursting with a zest for life. The coffee tastes wonderful. And the honey and the marmalade. We go out into the sunshine, sniffing the warm, friendly air. I rejoice in the new day.

"You know," I say to Anne, "after an experience like the one last night, one will no longer be the same. Do you know what I believe is the greatest danger to a couple in love?"

"Tell me."

"Clinging to each other. It has a detrimental effect on the one who is clinging and extinguishes the love of the one who is being clung to."

"I couldn't agree more."

"Not until you have experienced that you are alone on this earth—only then, I think, can you start to belong."

Consciousness need not be a product of the brain, nor be IN the brain.

Stanislav Grof

I belong. I feel that I belong. I feel it in my body. I no longer have the sensation of being isolated. I have always given my women friends a hug whenever I felt like it. Now I also hug my male friends. The reactions have amazed me. From surprise to shyness. Some people are moved, overwhelmed, grateful, pleased—never disgusted.

° ° °

Do we have a consciousness that is independent of the body? If so, is this consciousness a part of a greater consciousness, a web of consciousness that embraces existence as a whole, in the same way as the minute units on physics—particles and waves—appear to be parts of an interwoven web of the entire universe?

° ° °

I have tried to describe experiences in non-ordinary states of consciousness to some "accountants." "It's only chemistry," they said.

I replied, "Would you stop listening to a symphony on TV or a compact disc and say it was only electronics?"

As long as we are in our bodies, we are chemical beings, and changes in our chemistry create changes in our "receiver." For that matter, how do we know that our brain isn't like a TV set? The music and the pictures are neither in, nor are they being created by the apparatus. This merely transmits waves from the outside.

The many documented out-of-body experiences are indications of the fact that we have a consciousness that is independent of the body. For example: at the same time a person is lying apparently dead on the operating table, he can see himself and everything in the room from above, and hear what is being said. The consciousness can even move along the hall and into other rooms in the hospital. When the person describes what he has heard and seen in other rooms, after coming back to life and everyday consciousness, it may be verified exactly by those who were there. How can this be? The body and the brain were not on an outing. Only a form of consciousness was.

There are also cases of totally blind people who have been able to see everything, even in color, during out-of-body experiences.

Mechanistic science finds it difficult to accept such phenomena. But what kind of science is this if it ignores certain observations, instead of regarding them as a challenge?

If we change the electronics of the TV apparatus, the pictures we see change. But they were out there on the wave bands all the time. Perhaps our "pictures" are also there. It is simply a question of adjusting the channel selector (i.e., changing the chemical processes in the brain so that we are able to see them). But if this is true, who is sending the signals?

Aldous Huxley had this to say about such chemistry: "The way to the superconscious is through the subconscious, and the way, or at least one of the ways, to the subconscious is through the chemistry of individual cells."

° ° °

If we have a consciousness that is detached from the body, that exists independently of the body, has it existed both before and after the lifetime of the body?

Reincarnation—the idea that the human soul is not restricted to the life of a single body—is one of the oldest and most comprehensive beliefs of mankind.

A friend of mine told the following story, which I have every reason to believe is true:

Many years ago he was driving with his three-year-old son. As they went past an old house, the son said, "I used to live in that house." And pointed to it.

"No," said the father, "We've never lived there."

"Oh yes," said the son. "I lived there. My name was Nils. I was married to a lady named Grete, and we had nine children."

The father was amused by this, but he didn't take his son very seriously. Nevertheless, he couldn't resist the temptation to check old archives. It was true. During the previous century, a man named Nils had lived in that house. He had a wife named Grete, and they had nine children.

° ° °

I am willing to believe that the Duchess and a number of other experiences that I have described were transmissions from previous lives because of the intense emotions connected with them, and because the discharge of these emotions produced such a marked change in my mental state. Reliving the experience of being hanged put a definite end to the stiff neck that I always had. Would this mean that we carry the experiences from previous lives in our unconscious?

In his files at the University of Virginia, Ian Stevenson, a professor of psychiatry, has collected more than two thousand case histories that suggest reincarnation. He has specialized in cases in which children, both in the East and in the West, have spontaneous, detailed recollections of what they believe to be previous lives. Through on-the-spot investigations and interviews with witnesses, he has checked out as many of the stories as possible. Not infrequently, he interviewed as many as twenty-five people in a single case.

Stevenson likes to work with children between the ages of two and four. It appears as if children of this age are still open to memories that may be from other lives. They are able to provide the most incredible details about people, cities, houses, clothing, jewelry, weapons, etc. This is a knowledge which is impossible for such a young child to have obtained in this life. Another advantage of working with little children is that their previous lives ended so recently that there are greater opportunities for checking what they say.

A little child might say, "When I was old...," "When I was eighty...," "Before I was born," etc. However, it doesn't take long before the memories fade, and by the ages of five to eight as a rule, they are gone.

Stevenson also leaves room for the possibility that these reminiscences may be genetically inherited, an indication that the child is in touch with the collective unconscious; or that these are telepathic results, tuned into the mind of a living person. His conclusion is that there is strong evidence that reincarnation occurs, enough perhaps for a rational person to believe, but not conclusive proof.

It appears as if phobias may be remnants of previous lives. The same is true of talents. There are a number of examples of little children who appear to have the same skills as the persons they point out as "themselves" in previous lives. This is true of other personality traits as well.

Stevenson recalls a child with hydrophobia who remember her death in a previous life. It happened when she was standing on a bridge and stepped back in order to let a bus pass. She fell in the water and was drowned. In her current life she had a phobic fear of buses, bridges and water. Five adults had to hold her down in order to give her a bath.

Another of Stevenson's case histories is an out-and-out detective story:

A two-and-half-year-old child gave a glass of water to a guest who was visiting the family. Afterwards, when he was told to remove the empty glass, he said, to everyone's amazement, "I won't do it. I am the son of a Sharma." (a high caste in India) He became angry and broke several glasses.

The boy's name was Gopal Gupta. He lived in Delhi with his parents, who had modest educations. He was asked to explain his impolite behavior. He said he had previously lived in Mathura, where he had servants to remove glasses.

He spoke of his former father and two brothers. His youngest brother had killed him by shooting him in the chest. He had also had a bitter argument with his former wife. Gopal mentioned that he had owned a well-known medical supply firm.

These facts, and many others that came out later, were gradually verified. Of forty-six facts recorded by Stevenson in the case, only one was partially incorrect, whilc it was impossible to verify three.

When the former family—which was rich and well-educated—heard rumors about the boy in Delhi who claimed that he had once lived with them, several members came to meet him. First his former wife, a sister and her son, and then his older brother. Gopal identified them all. He also recognized another sister, although with greater difficulty.

This sister invited Gopal to a wedding in another town, and there he suddenly stood face to face with the younger brother who had killed him. The brother had been sentenced to life imprisonment but had been released because of ill health. Gopal greeted him by name at once.

Gopal had already revealed that the motive for the murder was that his younger brother—who had been drinking heavily—had considerable debts and needed money. At that time it had not been possible to advance the brother a loan. A quarrel had arisen and a shot was fired.

Not until he was nine years old did Gopal visit Mathura and his old home. He also visited his former wife. When Gopal had met her in Delhi for the first time, his father had noticed that he was very reserved with her. In the presence of several people, Gopal now informed them that, when his younger brother had asked him for money, he had tried to help him by borrowing five thousand rupees from his wife. She had refused.

At this revelation, the lady fainted. When she came to again she denied the circumstances. Later, however, she had plucked up courage and confessed that Gopal was telling the truth. When Stevenson asked for her permission to publish this case, she willingly gave it to him.*

For a number of years, as part of a scientific research project, Dr. Helen Wambach has hypnotized several thousand adults, and produced reminiscences that may be

---

*The two above-mentioned cases have been taken from *Reincarnation - A New Horizon in Science, Religion and Society* by Sylvia Cranston and Carney Williams, Julian Press, New York, 1984.

best understood as coming from previous lives. These cover periods that extend over many centuries. Today, a number of psychiatrists and psychologists are using this kind of recollected material with their patients in the treatment of psychic illnesses.

° ° °

The most interesting question in connection with reincarnation is, of course, whether evidence—if one is to interpret it as such—of a previous life is also evidence of a future life.

Michael Grosso has written about this: "Still, evidence for backward continuity would enhance antecedent probability of forward continuity. The fact that something of 'me' was around before my body appeared on the scene makes it easier to believe that something of 'me' will be around after it is gone."

Conversely, if one rejects the idea of previous lives, but believes in resurrection (i.e., that the soul has an eternal life after this), one may ask: Does it really sound logical that the non-physical part of a person should be created out of nothingness during the physical conception? Should it, during the physical existence, develop a potential for eternal life? "That a human mind emerges at birth along with a particular body, and yet manages to escape dissolution at the time of bodily death, seems at least curiously asymmetrical," Grosso philosophizes.

Well, what are we to believe? To me, the pieces fall into place—what I have experienced has coherence—if I regard this in the light of reincarnation.

Obviously, these transpersonal pictures, this part of my unconscious which has no basis in my present life, may be expressions of the collective unconscious, my access to all consciousness at all times. From the point of view of immortality, however, it makes little difference. As the Benedictine monk said, "It is not a question of reincarnation or not, but of *what* is reincarnating." What he meant was: Do we remain "individuals" all the time or does "everyone reincarnate in everyone?"

° ° °

When it comes to the natural sciences, it is apparent that the most advanced thinkers today reject the fact that life consists solely of chemical reactions and physical manifestations. Also among these sciences that are concerned with "measuring things," it is maintained that life and consciousness must consist of dimensions above and beyond those we know today.

Rupert Sheldrake is a British biologist and biochemist with a Ph.D. from Cambridge and a Research Fellow of the Royal Society. In his revolutionary books, *A New Science of Life* and *The Presence of the Past*, he concludes that living organisms are not simply complex biological machines, and that life cannot be reduced to chemical reactions.

Sheldrake points out that science has been unable to explain the fundamental question of why living organisms—human beings, animals, plants—receive their special shapes and behavior. The fact is that the same molecular basis of heredity, DNA, with identical genetic material, proteins and chemical compounds, becomes a leg in one instancc, and an arm in another instance. How does this occur?

He believes that information is very likely transmitted by other channels than through the genes. He develops the idea of "morphogenetic fields": that there is a "memory" inherent in nature that "transmits" information, independent of time and space and physical transference. And he asks the question of whether the laws of nature are as final as we have believed. Perhaps they are undergoing constant evolution like everything else in the universe? Perhaps they are gradually being shaped by "habits" among the different organisms as these develop? And that there is a "memory" of these habits that determines the further shape, behavior and development of the species.

Experiments have been made in training rats to learn specific tricks. It has been ascertained that this has made it remarkably easier to train rats in an entirely different country to learn the same tricks. How has the learning ability been transmitted? Not through the genes. It is here Sheldrake suggests the "morphogenetic field" as a means of transmission.

Perhaps the same is true of human beings. When a technical or cultural conquest occurs in one place on earth, the same phenomena crop up in other places, without there necessarily having been any "factual" communication. The transmission must have taken place in another dimension which has not yet been recognized by the mechanistic sciences. Can we call this a dimension of consciousness?

° ° °

In the field of physics a total change in paradigms has taken place during the last decades. Not many years have gone by since physicists believed that the universe of matter was composed of tiny units that could be measured. If only matter could be broken down into these building blocks, an exact definition and determination of the laws of nature could be made.

But then it turned out that even smaller units were inside what were thought to be the final building blocks, until one arrived at infinitely tiny particles or waves that were not especially willing to let themselves be defined or measured. The fact is that when attempts were made to measure them, it turned out that the results were influenced by the one who was doing the measuring. This and other things led to the conclusion that all matter inexplicably hangs together, like a web, and that it is not possible to isolate a single part and measure it separately. Particles and waves arise, disappear, change character. It may be estimated that, under ceratin conditions, they will probably behave in one way or another, but this cannot be established with any certainty.

In his book, *The Tao of Physics*, physicist Fritjof Capra says:

"Quantum theory thus reveals a basic oneness of the universe. It shows that we cannot decompose the world into independently existing smallest units. As we penetrate into matter, nature does not show us any isolated 'basic building blocks,' but rather appears as a complicated web of relations between the various parts of the whole. These relations always include the observer in an essential way... This means that the classical ideal of an objective description of nature is no longer valid."

Stanislav Grof has collected a wealth of material from the journeys of people in altered states of consciousness, on which he has based his epoch-making teachings and doctrines. Like Sheldrake, he tries to build a bridge between the world of natural science and the non-material world. In his book, *Beyond the Brain*, State University of New York Press, 1985, he writes:

"The concept of the cosmos as a gigantic supermachine, assembled from countless separate objects and existing independently from the observer, has become obsolete and has been relegated to the historical archives of science. The updated model shows the universe as a unified and indivisible web of events and relationships; its parts represent different aspects and patterns of one integral process of unimaginable complexity... As scientists have probed into the deepest structure of matter and studied the multifarious aspects of the processes in the world, the notion of solid substance has gradually disappeared from the picture, leaving them only with archetypal patterns, abstract mathematical formulas, or universal order."

It has been possible to confirm many transpersonal experiences in unusual states of consciousness. People have described places and events, individuals and clothing from previous centuries, with a knowledge of details impossible for them to have acquired in this life. Later, by historical research it has been established that their descriptions tally with probable living conditions. People have even spoken foreign or extinct languages that have been totally unknown to them.

Grof seriously discusses "the possibility that the connecting principle in the cosmic web is consciousness as a primary and further irreducible attribute of existence."

Here he is in the company of leading physicists. David Bohm describes the universe as a living organism, of which the organs, tissues and cells have meaning only in relation to the whole. This, he says, includes both the phenomena we experience through our senses and with the help of scientific instruments, which he believes are only a fragment of reality and the total existence. This, in turn, is filled with meaning which gives rise to the consciousness.

Capra points out that there are clear parallels between modern physics and Eastern mysticism. He shows how both perceive everything in the universe as being interconnected. The world view of the Eastern mystics is that things in their fundamental nature are not nameable or explicable. They cannot be adequately expressed in any form of language. For this reason, the Eastern sages are generally not interested in explaining things, but, rather in having a spontaneous, non-intellectual experience of the unity of all things. This is precisely what happened to me during my inner journeys.

Along with physicist Geoffrey Chew, Capra arrives at the conclusion that, "the existence of consciousness, along with all other aspects of nature, is necessary for self-consistency of the whole." Capra writes: "This view, again, is in perfect harmony with the views of the Eastern mystical traditions which have always regarded consciousness as an integral part of the universe. In the Eastern view, human beings, like all other life forms, are parts of an inseparable organic whole. Their intelligence, therefore, implies that the whole, too, is intelligent."

Grof writes: "In some sense, if the universe represents an integral and unified web and some of its constituents are obviously conscious, this must be true for the entire system."

And he arrives at the following conclusion which, for me, represents one of the fundamental conclusions in consciousness research: "The experiential insights from unusual states of consciousness suggest the existence of an intangible and unfathomable creative intelligence aware of itself that permeates all realms of reality. This approach indicates that it is pure consciousness without any specific content that represents the supreme principle of existence and the ultimate reality."

° ° °

Is consciousness, then, a product of the brain? Materialistic science claims that it is. It is possible to cut into the brain and create "distortions in the consciousness processes." But this does not prove that consciousness is produced in the brain. This is a mechanistic way of thinking—I believe only in what I can cut into. Think of the parallel of the TV set. The TV repairman "cuts into" the receiving apparatus. He does not change the programs that are transmitted.

Wilder Penfield—a neurosurgeon who has made basic contributions to modern neurophysiology—has written a book called *The Mystery of the Mind.* Here he expresses considerable doubt about the consciousness being a part of the brain and being explainable with the help of cerebral anatomy and physiology.

According to Grof: "At the same time as people are bodies with organic functions, we also function as unlimited fields of consciousness, that transcend matter, space, time and linear causality."

An open mind is the foremost indication of intelligence.

° ° °

What are the conclusions that may be drawn from this? What does this mean to us ordinary people who are trying to answer the questions: Who am I? Where am I going? What happens to me behind the mysterious door called "Death"?

If we regard ourselves as an isolated, biological "machine," then death is obviously the final disaster. But if we accept the fact that we are part of the great web, and build on experiences from unusual states of consciousness, we may be able to regard death as the reunion with a wholeness beyond our comprehension.

° ° °

The instruments of science do not go very far. For this reason, some have realized that it is possible to use thought itself as the tool to search with. The spontaneous, "unconscious" thought. As early as 1936, Albert Einstein declared that the progress of physics was not due to new measurements but to free insight.

The Russian and American cosmologists, Linde and Guth, among others, have launched a cosmology in which our universe is a tiny part of an even greater whole. According to this theory, universes like our own are born and die. A gross analogy might be to imagine a kettle of boiling water, in which bubbles are rising and disappearing all the time—and each is a universe.

Would we be able to enter and study other universes in detail with thought alone? Because with the astronomical windows at our disposal, we are reduced to studying the rays of light of the past in our universe.

What is it then that causes a universe to emerge? The fact that the creation occurs in the form of our own, well-known Big Bang? With our thought we can imagine—without being able to measure it—that a universe emerges when a field has sufficient density and energy. But it may also be imagined that the sum of all energy in a universe is equal to zero (mc, which means the content of the mass-energy is positive, and the gravitational energy is negative, and that they therefore neutralize each other).

If so, this means that a universe may be created out of nothing or, at any rate, that nothing material is needed. Can it be created from consciousness?

He, who has no contact with his spiritual self, does not really know himself.

Stanislav Grof

Eva is a young, unmarried woman whom I met during this period. For years she had been suffering from depression, moodiness and pent-up aggression. At the same time she presented a gentle, amenable face to her surroundings. She was continually haunted by feelings of guilt. She felt that everything that went wrong in the family was her fault.

Eva is a very intelligent and gifted person who is not content with superficiality. With considerable willpower, she is determined to assume responsibility for her life and do something about it. Up to now, she had been unable to find a way. She was struggling with a veritable identity crisis, or, to use my expression: Who am I? Now she had heard about holotropic therapy. In this connection we came in contact.

We talked together several times until we knew each other well. Then we tried two holotropic sessions, with hyperventilation and music. Afterwards she wrote a report for her own reference. I have been given permission to quote from it here.

"My first experience during an inner journey was on board a ship, a large cruise ship. I see myself as a woman, quite elegant. I am accustomed to getting whatever I want. I am there with my husband and several children. A very romantic marriage, I believe. A passionate love between man and woman.

"My husband and I are in our cabin. It is a lovely cabin, in light colors—blue and cream. We have just made love, and the woman (it is important to understand that *I* am the woman) is standing before a mirror in a white slip, I think. He is still in bed. Then comes the accident! I think it has something to do with water. There seems to be water everywhere. I feel quite alone and there is a lot of panic around me.

"It all seems inconceivable. I cannot understand what is happening. I am terribly frightened, and have never experienced such a brutal shock. What a contrast to everything that had been so idyllic—the romance, the wonderful beauties with my husband and children. But I don't think about this until afterwards, because in the midst of the disaster I don't believe that I thought about anything. I knew there were many people in the same situation, and they were all trying to save themselves.

"Then I see the woman—me—from behind, sitting on the edge of a bed. There are other people in the room: several children and, to the right, a man in a uniform like those worn by the staff of a hotel and waiters. He places a hand on my shoulder and says something, but I do not seem to hear. I feel as if I have sunk into a deep black hole. I experience a grief that I never knew existed, a grief so great that I am unable to conceive of why or how I will be able to go on living. I know that I have lost a child and my husband. It is too much, and I withdraw into myself. But I know that everyone assumes that I will be strong, as always.

"The next few days after this inner journey, I felt a terribly helpless anger. The woman knew that there was nothing she could do to bring back those she had lost. She blamed herself for the loss of the child, for not looking after him when the accident occurred. She felt responsible for it.

"After this experience, I know what it means to be overwhelmed by grief. I have never experienced anything like this during my life. So where it came from I do not know.

"The second session was about a woman whom I again experience as myself (the emotions, the thoughts, everything in me). She is around forty, has grey wispy hair. She is wearing a faded, worn, greyish sprigged muslin dress. It hangs loosely about her like a sack. She is very thin, has my features, and looks old. She has been exposed to torture for a long time. The pain has made her a little mad, not unlike these 'bag ladies.' But she is also very strong. She knows that she will never be able to convey to anyone how truly gruesome it is.

"The woman is in a kind of concentration camp, and I/she see(s) dead bodies lying in a big open square. The square is surrounded by a wall. In the middle of one side there is a kind of wooden gate. When I cross the square, with dead bodies around me, I am aware of the sleazy dress hanging loosely on my body. This is no new sight; I have seen it many times before. But it is so inconceivably macabre, so totally incomprehensible that people are capable of doing so much devilment to each other.

"It is hell, and I know that neither a film nor photographs can convey how gruesome it is. I'll never get over it.

"The woman harbors thoughts of revenge, particularly that she will carry everything she experiences with her to the grave.

"The uniformed people who guard me non-stop can finish me off in a flash. But I have been through so much that I no longer feel any fear. I am beyond fear because I have a very strong faith in God. No matter what deviltry they do, God will triumph, and they will never be able to crush me. I seize every opportunity to say something about faith. I feel such an inner strength through this woman. I have a conviction which I neither possess nor feel in my everyday life. The woman refuses point-blank to give up and is as tough as shoe leather, no matter what they do.

"I think the worst thing for her is to see how young and insecure the ones in power are. She knows there is hope for them if they dare shake off the mask of power, and feel more. All the horrible things that occur here are the result of ignorance. Perhaps a few of them like what she says, when they are alone with her, but outwardly they will never reveal that her constant preaching about love has any effect on them.

"I know now that we belong to something greater, of which we are a part and are helping to create. I experience an intensely powerful faith. No matter what they did to me, it made no difference. It was their stupidity that made them incapable of seeing the light and the love.

"After these experiences I felt so extremely well and so secure and was filled with joy. I felt that I accepted myself completely. I realize now that there is so much more to us than we think, and that we have the answer within ourselves. It almost goes without saying that we are divine in a way.

"It has become easier to grasp the very core of me. It is as if I am able to go in there. The little me, who never likes to be out in the light, who feels completely naked, who wriggles out of everything, the loneliest, the real me, has been so completely hidden for many years. I have overplayed it, become lonelier and lonelier, concealed the voice from within, done everything to keep from hearing it. Now it is easier for me to find this part of me, an intense feeling of warmth filling my body, I feel embarrassed, but I let the little one be exposed to the light. I know I mustn't shut myself up again, even if I start to cry, not isolate myself even if it is unpleasant. Be alone long enough, allow it to live, give it time."

° ° °

What kind of experiences were these? They lay within her, just below the surface. Were they carried over from previous lives? Were they from her "collective unconscious"? Was it a symbolic language for birth? From a therapeutic point of view it does not matter very much. Most important is the fact that Eva experienced these events, and the emotions that were connected with them. "This is heavy stuff!" she kept repeating during the sessions. She had never before experienced such intensely strong feelings.

The decisive factor is that Eva had the courage to "turn off her brain," go into her unconscious and bring this out into the open. In the second place, by experiencing this so realistically, as if it were happening here and now, she took the emotional charge out of these unconscious pictures. And by getting rid of the emotional charge, she was released from the burden they had been to her throughout the years. She had a difficult time during the succeeding period, when she integrated this material into her conscious life. We had long talks about this.

It wasn't trifles she had carried with her. How *could* she be carefree and happy with this overwhelming material of fate inside her? She *had* to go in and experience it again. Nothing else had helped her, despite the fact that she had done considerable work with the problems of her childhood.

One remarkable discovery in these two sessions is her renewed faith in God. Eva said afterwards that she had always had a spiritual yearning, but it had been "overshadowed," as she put it, by the fact that the teachings of the church had been imposed upon her. It had become a "matter of conscience" without spiritual content. During these experiences her faith in God, or a Divine Power inside herself, had given her the strength to survive. This has opened the door to tremendous resources in her. But, as she said, "It is not the faith as preached by the Church. This did not evoke any holy or divine feelings in me."

Eva's concern for and understanding of the people in power who tortured her are worth noticing. She felt pity for them, "for they know not what they do."

The second session ended with several happy experiences, in which Eva was with a tribe of Indians who had long black hair. She was one of them, and they rode on horses in a beautiful brownish landscape, where peace and harmony prevailed. Eva was very happy. As she said, "A natural, inevitable happiness."

We decided to stop there for the time being.

Afterwards, I remained in touch with her for a year. She went to New York where she is training wholeheartedly as an actress. She seems happy, and has acquired new self-confidence.

...the battle between world views is a battle between different kinds of experiences that people have, and that they think are real, true and clear. If materialism prevails today, it may be less a sign of its truth than of the limitations in the sorts of experiences people are having.

Michael Grosso

If it is true that we return to this planet again and again, why do we return to fight one another? Wage war? Why all this violence? Why do people have so much aggression in themselves?

Do we carry so much aggression, fear and insecurity, hate and suspicion in our unconscious? And if this is true, where does it come from? Transpersonal psychology, which goes hand in hand with consciousness research, has shown that what we have "acquired" of these doubtful qualities after we came into this world—as a rule—correspond to only a part of the amount we carry around with us.

The "unhappy childhood" is undoubtedly significant, but this is not the main reason. The root of the evil is to be found in the traumas of birth and in transpersonal material. Unless one goes into the part of the unconscious in which the imprint of the birth—and even earlier material—are to be found, it is not possible to untie these knots totally and effectively. Sexual abnormalities may have their roots here as well.

Stanislav Grof is convinced that much of our aggression arises during the process of birth. The phase in which the mother is struggling to push out the child—a struggle that appears to be even more painful and dramatic to the child than to the mother—is experienced by the child as a struggle to survive.

Later, during inner journeys in an unusual state of consciousness, when a person relives the trauma of birth more or less directly or symbolically, these stored energies are gradually discharged. According to Grof, this may be experienced symbolically as violent scenes of war, from brutal battles among cave dwellers to Star Wars, revolutions, nuclear explosions, natural catastrophes, volcanic eruptions, earthquakes, tornados. Archetypical themes may include Doomsday, Purgatory and mythological pictures of struggles between demons and angels, titans and gods.

Symbolically or directly—in addition to aggression, the emotions that are activated and brought to the surface, include self-destructive impulses, fear, violent sexual excitement and various bodily pains. But gradually, as the delivery approaches, the spiritual self is also awakened.

I remember from my very first session of hyperventilation: After breathing for an hour, I experienced a total obstruction of my throat. I felt that I was choking, I was unable to speak, I couldn't utter a sound, nor breathe. My Australian friend, who was sitting with me, called Stanislav Grof.

"Birth!" said Stan. "Do you want to get rid of it?"

I nodded.

"Lie on your stomach," he said.

I turned over. Stan, who at the time probably weighed over 200 pounds, sat on my back. Both he and my Australian friend, who is no featherweight either, leaned over my back and shoulders, and pressed me down on the floor.

"Push up!" said Stan. It was impossible. It was so painful that it is indescribable. "Powerful! Powerful!" Stan shouted.

I pushed. Up against the two of them. The pain penetrated the sound barrier. It was as if I exceeded the limits of my endurance. I was seized with the wildest panic, a frenzy of rage, squeezed together, wedged in. And I pushed, in all probability with much greater energy than I usually possess. And then came the scream. I screamed! I screamed as I have never screamed. Screamed all the pain, the tension, the aggression out of me. And then it let go its hold. I collapsed, exhausted. My throat cleared. I was able to breathe. I could speak. I was through. I calmed down.

Unfortunately, it was too late to check with my mother whether I had been born with the umbilical cord around my neck. I remember as a child growing up how I sometimes had tensions in my throat that caused me to stutter and made it difficult for me to speak. After this experience, the tensions were gone forever. Contrary to popular belief, stammering can be cured.

I was not the only one who had to go through the nightmare. Around me, other people were screaming. Many were crying. Some were thrashing wildly about. The music was deafening. It was an inferno. I jotted down the following:

> There are so many tears
> in this world
> if all the tears
> came out of us
> what an ocean
> it would be...

Gratefully, I lay on my back and continued my hyperventilation. Now there was a period in which I went into a different state of consciousness and lay completely still with my experience at the inner level.

I also remember another strange episode during a later session. I experienced that I was a fetus. I lay curled up like the fetus with one hand on my head. I *was* the fetus, and it was a wonderful state. Suddenly my fingers caught hold of the hairs on my head, and I didn't understand a thing. I thought: What on earth? Such long hair! How can my hair be so long? I lay tugging at it in amazement. And slowly I returned to my everyday consciousness.

I would also like to tell about a third dramatic birth experience. Well into a non-ordinary state of consciousness, I experienced being a woman in labor. I lay on my back and struggled with labor pains. I experienced the pains, but also the expectation, and a strange sexual stimulation. When the time came for the delivery, I didn't know whether I was the one who was giving birth, or the one who was being born. The ecstacy was the same.

What does such an experience mean? Is it a transmission from a former life as a woman, or is it the strong impression of the birth in me that manifests itself in various ways? It makes little difference. The "delivery" took place in any case.

There is no doubt that someone who relives the titanic struggle of birth in an unusual state of consciousness (and one is seldom finished with it in a single session) gets rid of much of his pent-up aggression. But something more happens: a death and rebirth occur. Experiencing birth is like dying, and in order to be reborn, first one must die.

Grof says: "The critical turning point in the process of inner transformation is ego-death and the conceptual destruction of the individual's old world."

What does he mean by "ego-death"? It is difficult to understand that you can die and yet live. You have to die to the false self-system, your ego, built on lies, before a new self can be born. To undergo the ego-death is such a strong crisis that your ego—the picture you have of yourself—is destroyed. It entails an instant merciless destruction of every previous point of reference in your life. The ego-consciousness with which we perceive our surroundings, verging on intolerance, what we experience and cling to as our "I"—all of this is crushed, annihilated, collapses like a house of playing cards, dies. This means letting go of conceptions of the past—the attitudes, faith, identity, success, ties to people, places, roles, even stability itself if it is based on lies. It is extremely painful, but it is an incredible cleansing process, a fire that consumes everything.

Then, out of the ashes like the Phoenix arises a new "I-concept," a mind that is more open, more confident, more tolerant, more considerate of others, interested, willing to relax the control and admit higher forces. In other words, a richer person. The one who previously went about restlessly, without peace, without harmony—with an indefinable fear, without the ability to love—will experience a new world in and around oneself. And understand that the old ego was built on lies, self-deception and deceit. He or she will be able to enjoy the simple pleasures of everyday life—love, work, play, music, art and nature. He will be able to live for others.

° ° °

Tonight I awoke abruptly with a strange "vision." I "saw" that all life originates from one cell. And that this cell was pure, without pollution. I "saw" that all of us, all life, is in this one cell.

I "saw" that every life-form, biological life and thought life, is in this cell and that the ingredient of the cell is light. LIGHT!

I "saw" that all life in this cell may choose—darkness or light. Break down—or keep it clean for itself. Break down—or keep it clean for itself.

The sight was overwhelming. It is not easy to describe it in words. I "saw" how the cell struggles to survive. And that we must choose Light!

I realize now that this was the intention of the Luminous Being during our first encounter when she begged me to say "Yes" to life. She wanted me to choose Light.

I remain awake for the rest of the night, thinking: What does it mean for *my* life, in every aspect, to every person, to choose Light?

I close my eyes and see a tiny flickering candle at the end of the tunnel. So this is what is going to lead me, what I must protect. It had almost blown out.

° ° °

Anne is still asleep. She always sleeps so quietly. She lies on her back, breathing calmly through her nose. Now I have time to study her face undisturbed. Her beautiful face. So familiar and so strange. What is she dreaming about just now? What do *her* inner worlds look like?

"Soul-mate" is a common phrase these days. Implying: The only one. The choice of one's heart. The other half of oneself, for whom we are always yearning and searching. Since we were divided in two at the dawn of time.

Are Anne and I soul-mates? True soul-mates? The soul is eternal. Then soul-mates must be bound eternally as mates. For all time. But soul-mates are not necessarily ready for each other. One or both of them has something to learn first. Does such a perspective exceed the individual life cycle? Who knows?

Anne awakens. "Hello dear," she says before she opens her eyes. She has felt my eyes on her. In the morning, the moment we open our eyes, the sun is always shining, the sky is blue, and the water is pure and clear so we can see the colorful stones.

I run my finger along the bridge of her nose. "The Duchess!"

She laughs. "Duchesses are not to be trifled with."

"There are so few of them."

"Be happy about that."

I tell her about my "vision." "Do you believe that it can be true that all life originates from one cell, that it contains the kernel of everything?"

"If you saw it. It may also be that in the macrocosmos our planet is one cell, Gaia, and that it was this cell you saw?"

"The worst thing was the way we are poisoning it. The lower half was infested with dark forces. And they are eating their way up. If it doesn't stop, it will die."

"What was the time perspective?"

"I don't know. This was beyond time."

Anne looks at me thoughtfully. "If you can wake up with a vision like this, it is probably because the door to your inner world has been opened during your 'journeys.' And now it is standing open. During the moment between sleep and the waking state, at any rate."

"Yes. I go in and out." I close my eyes, try to go back into the vision. "The pollution is terrible," I say. "Not only are we destroying ourselves, but we are also razing nature and the other life-forms on this planet. Instead of realizing that we are one with them, in the same cell. To feel that you are one with the other forms of life is the first step on the way to protecting them."

"It is said that the Earth breathes."

"The Indians, and other so-called primitive peoples, revere nature because it is alive. Rivers and mountains, stones and trees, animals and seas, everything is alive, and thus is sacred. The materialistic person only wishes to *exploit* nature for money. He sees no mystery to marvel at. He has no respect."

"They say we are approaching a global near-death experience. Perhaps this is necessary if the spiritual dimension of man is to be re-awakened."

"Yes. Drought? Nuclear catastrophe? Pollution of the oceans? The fact that the ozone layers are disappearing? I hope the near-death experience is only 'near.' It appears as if strong medicine is needed if humankind is to see something other than itself."

"If only we had seen ourselves. Every dimension of ourselves. Then things wouldn't have gone so wrong."

"I think the tragedy of mankind is that we think we are the greatest. This is why we lack respect. Those who have experienced unusual states of consciousness have learned that something much, much greater exists. It is only a question of having access to it. This is why inner journeys and meditation are so important. We do not become *whole* until we have united ourselves with our inner world, the spiritual side of ourselves."

"Huxley said something to the effect that merely a fleeting experience of what 'God is love' really means would shake society to its foundations."

"We have this spiritual force in us, 'The God within.' The reason why our materialistic world is so sick is because we have closed the way to this spiritual force."

"This is caused by fear," says the wise Anne.

"What are we humans so afraid of?"

"The unknown, I would think."

"Always the unknown. But then we must expand the limits of what is known!" I suggest.

Anne gets up. "I'm hungry. Will you make the coffee?"

"Yes, but not too strong."

I love our philosophical discussions in the mornings. I follow Anne into the bathroom, still haven't had enough. I stand behind her and run my hands down her perfect body. "Here you are whole, at any rate."

"Being whole also means experiencing that we are all both masculine and feminine," she says. "That we have both energies inside us."

"That would put an end to the struggle between the sexes."

"The destructive at any rate. The feminine in the man can help him open the door to his spiritual world and his unconscious. The masculine in the woman can give her strength to master life."

"In the karmic perspective it is probably true that we alternate between being man and woman."

"I'm glad that we have become what we are this time," she says, and gives me a hug.

"Pure consciousness is without sex," I say. "I experienced this myself. It is only when it settles in a body that we choose sex."

The coffee was just right. The farewell is drawing near.

"How does *your* day look?" I ask.

The first cloud is covering the sun.

"Busy," she says. "This and that."

"Will you be interviewing anyone?"

"That, too."

"Perhaps you'll be late?"

"You may count on that."

I ask no more questions. I was asking out of interest. But perhaps it sounded like controlling.

The day passes. In the morning I work well. But the afternoon is long. It is a new experience for me to be the one at home, while the other one goes out. If I had understood how necessary it was for the one at home to share the life out there, when I myself went out, I might have done a better job in my previous marriages.

At last I hear her car door slam. She comes in with her arms full of bags. I put them on the kitchen table. She has been to the farm and bought vegetables. We try a vegetarian week.

She sniffs. "What are you making?"

"Soup. With carrots, celery, onions, potatoes, tomatoes, mushrooms and green peppers."

"Heavens!"

"And cucumbers, thyme and dill. How was your day?"

"Good."

"Did you get everything done?"

"Yes."

"Met any interesting people?" I can hear myself hassling her.

"Some."

I feel a knot in my stomach. I *mustn't* ask any more questions. "Anything come of it?"

"It was interesting."

"Something you can use for the television program?"

"I don't know."

"But you seem satisfied, at any rate."

I wait.

Anne lifts the lid of the pot. "We may have to heat it up."

"I'll do it."

Is it because she knows that I expect her to tell me, that she is unable to?

"I haven't been out of the door," I say. "Been writing and reading the whole day."

"Good."

"I read Joseph Campbell on myths. The sign that one is heading in the right direction is the feeling of bliss."

A brief pause. I continue, "Did you feel that way today?"

She looks at me. "I *will* tell you," she says. "Only you must give me time!"

° ° °

Share everything, or each one live his or her own life?

The feeling of freedom. This is *my* life. Without accounting to anyone, without being controlled.

Two different attitudes toward life, I should think. Two different needs.

Does it all boil down to this: The joy of giving? The gratitude of receiving? Without demanding. Respecting each other as he/she is?

° ° °

I have a beautiful vision of an elderly couple sitting on a bench, hand in hand, gazing at the same star.

And when they have finally gone to bed in the evening, she lifts aside her nightgown and says graciously, "You are still welcome, my dear."

The true journey of discovery
does not consist in finding
new landscapes, but in seeing
with new eyes.

Marcel Proust

It has been a hot summer, 90° F in the shade for several weeks. First we had a drought. Then we had a week of downpours. The river became broad. Anne and I play golf.

Anne has received her Ph.D. in psychology. We celebrate with a trip to the undulating, maple-clad Berkshire Mountains. There we stay in small inns in villages from the Colonial Period. We find local theaters with excellent performances. And concerts. It isn't necessary to go to New York.

We laugh and enjoy ourselves as in the old days. All is well as long as we don't try to possess each other. Not possess. No demand for rights, nothing that suffocates.

Anne *must* be free, must be able to *feel* free. She cannot live in any other way. This is a matter of life or death to her. It is my business to understand this. She must be able to live her own life. Every time we try to pretend that we are married, her uneasiness returns. I keep struggling to accept this, a tiny step every day.

"Anne, you are free! You are free!"

We are living in the present. And let the future emerge from that. There is no use *demanding* a future. If we are unable to give each other the present, we have no future in any case.

It was true that I had to give her up. I *am* renouncing her, I think, every single day.

But what conditions does this impose on love? Can it survive this? Or is it precisely this that makes it grow stronger?

° ° °

One day, while we are sitting at the breakfast table, Anne says, "I'm going away for a week."

"Oh?" I am accustomed to her going away for a few days. To seminars and courses. But a week is a bit long. "Where are you going?"

"I'll tell you when I come back."

"Oh?"

"I don't want you to be able to phone me. I have to be by myself for a while. There is something I have to find out."

"Well, well."

"I have to find again this feeling of freedom. I know you understand."

I think: The understanding may soon be used up.

"Are you going alone?" I ask. Exactly the opposite of what I had just decided.

"No."

Aha! Anne has many friends, of both sexes. We are faithful to each other, sexually. In fact, I assume that neither one of us desires anyone else. But there are other forms of intimacy.

"Am I permitted to ask who?"

"Yes, of course. I would have told you. I'm going with Joe."

Joe is her platonic, old psychologist friend. A man she has known for ten years, and with whom she talks shop. She has maintained a close contact with him all during our marriage. She can't let him go.

"*Must* you?"

"I need to talk with him. Besides, we're going to fast together. We don't even touch each other."

How jealous is one permitted to be? I say, "This is splitting up intimacy... The intimacy that is supposed to be reserved for one."

"Do you want to possess me again?"

How long will I be able to go on with this? Mustn't I soon tear her out of my heart? I get up and take plates and cups off the table. "Just go!"

She follows me. Stops in front of me.

"Yes, I must."

"I dare say consideration doesn't belong to your vocabulary."

"I beg of you to show consideration for me."

There is nothing more to say. During the next few days we live as before. But it is clear that it is murmuring beneath the surface. Inside me, at any rate. I start to tell myself that I no longer love this woman. That now I am longing for a good, old-fashioned, secure partnership. There must be limits to this freedom! *I* haven't any need to take a vacation with someone else. An author*ess* perhaps? I work myself up into a state. But I don't say anything. I *will* take a broad view of things.

The evening before she is to leave, we have guests. Two couples, close friends, one of the men a surgeon. We have eaten dinner and are sitting in front of the fireplace. It is past midnight. Anne is in the kitchen. We have a "country" kitchen that is a part of the living room. Suddenly we hear her cry, "Ow!"

She has cut herself on a glass she was wiping. The stem has broken. We come running. There is a deep, nasty cut. The surgeon decides that we must drive to the hospital where he can stitch it up.

Once there, we go past guards and receptionists, one behind the other like a family of ducks, straight into the operating room, the surgeon in front, then his wife, Anne and me. Anne lies down on the operating table. I stand beside her, and hold hear head. The surgeon gives her a local anesthetic, and opens and cleans and disinfects the cut. The blood flows. I think: This is all well and good. Anne is smart, lies with her head turned away. I, on the other hand, am unable to keep my eyes off the red, bloody flesh under the open skin. Out of character, I have been drinking quite a lot of wine this evening. I think: that is why I feel so strangely dizzy. I stroke Anne's forehead, and play the big hero. A cramp in my stomach makes it impossible for me to stand upright. The room whirls. I resist. I *will* not be weak. I continue to stroke her head. Then I hear myself saying, "I have to go to the toilet."

The next thing I know I am lying on my back on the floor of the corridor with six faces looking down at me. A doctor is taking my blood pressure, which appears to be zero. I try to get up because I want to go back into the operating room to comfort my wife, but they hold me down. I say, "There's nothing wrong with me. My blood pressure is perfect. Always has been. 120 over 80." But it doesn't help. They come with a bed on wheels. And I am forced to lie on it.

After a while, Anne's operation is over. Our friend, the surgeon, has taken thirty neat little sutures in Anne's neat little hand. My blood pressure is now 110 over 70, and we are allowed to go home.

Naturally, I am embarrassed. I can't understand how anything like this could happen to me. Fainting at the sight of a knife in a wound, and a little blood. I who have experienced so much, handled dead and wounded people during the war, for example. I make excuses to our friends. They comfort me. The surgeon's wife says, "It's different when you see it happening to someone you are fond of. Someone you love."

So I still love Anne? Is this the proof? I thought the fainting spell was due to the wine. I'd made up my mind to stick to that explanation.

We have gone to bed. I say to Anne, "You were quite heroic in there." She puts her arms around me.

"No, you were the hero," she says, "standing there, stroking my forehead until you lay on the floor." She kisses me and kisses me. "I love you. I love you," she repeats at least twenty times. I think, but I don't say it: Then stay with me! Why don't I say it? No.

The next morning I drive Anne to the airport. I only know that she is flying to a warmer place.

° ° °

It seems like an eternity since the Luminous Being appeared for the first time. Now she has become a daily companion. The Luminous Being is a cheerful being. She radiates joy from in there where she is to be found. She has a wonderful sense of humor, and we often chuckle together.

What does she look like? No, there are some secrets one must keep to oneself.

One thing is certain, the encounter with her has been an awakening. The bridge to the unconscious which she is.

° ° °

I say to Anne, "Now I am leaving this planet."

"Have a good trip," she says.

"I don't know if I am coming back."

"Good luck, then."

I find myself in a landscape of mosaics. Slowly I go through door after door. Around me are the most beautiful patterns, colors as clear as crystal, glittering precious stones, compositions that no human being could accomplish. The cathedrals and mosques and temples I have seen are only pale copies of this glorious magnificence.

The landscape is in the shape of a mandala, the circle that is the symbol of the totality of the Self. I know that I am at the source or origin of everything. Here are the answers to every question, as long as I am humble and wait. Yes, I can wait. It is as if I do not wish to hear the answers. They are not for me, not yet, the time is not ripe. I know that I will receive them, that I have them, they are in me.

Behind the next door I come to a white village. Houses, streets, people's clothing—everything is white. There are mules here. Anne comes towards me. A younger version of Anne. The people in the streets are happy. This is the village of love.

Then something staggering happens. A terrible catastrophe. I don't know what it is. It is greater and more terrible than the human mind is able to comprehend. A battle? A war? Total annihilation? Where is this? When is this? Is it in the future? What kind of destiny is this? Is it the end of mankind? Or is it the decline of another civilization? Is this the cause of man's deepest fear, the fear that is at the back of our unconscious soul, even after we have put the fear of death behind us?

I say to Anne, "This is greater than our life."

All the doors are open now. I feel the way strong forces begin to pull and tug at me. My body is making the strangest movements. I say, "Why am I behaving like this?"

Then the Luminous Being is standing there. She says, "Don't be afraid. Just come."

And I come. Into her realm.

Again I experience Africa. But who is coming toward me? The Black Goddess! I see only her face. It is round like a sun, and quite black. Her eyes are shining. Around her head is a glowing halo, like tongues of fire. But they are very yellow, a golden yellow. I do not speak to her. She does not speak to me.

I am a young man, running over the mountain with a girl. We are wearing strange leather clothing. We fling ourselves down in the heather and make love. Exuberant, giddy, abandoned love! Life! Uninhibited, unreserved, uncomplicated, simple times. What a wonderful life!

Now I am on board a ship. A sailing ship, in all likelihood a man-of-war. Difficult to date, but it is a wooden ship built of thick, heavy timber. I am down below. A battle is raging. I want to go out, but I must stay inside. The ship heels over, water pours in. I am drowning. But it is not terrible. Neither fear nor intense emotions are connected with this.

I am in a world of only animals. I am one of them. At one time I am an ape. I am animals I don't even recognize, that I have never heard of nor seen pictures of. Strange animals, with long necks and big heads, enormous humanlike eyes. Some are green, some are grey. One animal looks like an enormous caterpillar with an erect forepart. The body consists of many joints. Then I am a tiger or a lion. I lie curled up, with a huge paw on my head.

The images appear more rapidly. I am many different people—now a woman, now a man. Endlessly. I have previously experienced that *this* life has passed in review. Now it is as if many lives are passing in review, events from countless lives. My lives? The lives of others? On other planets? I do not know. The pictures crowd in so quickly and there are so many, that I can retain only a fraction of them. It is amazing. There is a wealth of material. With a flood of emotions.

Strange. All of this is in me. This multiplicity of pictures and situations, this is in me. It is as if the entire history of the planet Earth is inside me, emanating from the depths of my unconscious. In a strange way, I am one with it all. All of these lives. All of these people. From former times or future times. Of both sexes. The green fields, the trees, the animals. My world is expanding and expanding, out into the great void, out into infinity.

Then I understand—it comes like a bolt of lightning—the most fundamental epiphany: I AM NOTHING. This "I," this ego that I know, is nothing—in relation to the ocean of images in my depths with which I have come in contact.

I am this ocean, this is the real "me." The pictures and experiences and emotions there are affecting me, determining my attitudes, my actions. This is what governs me, what is *me*.

I am lying on my back, experiencing all of this. I am out of my body, but, at the same time, *in* my body. Because I feel pains in the small of my back. Suddenly I hear myself shouting: "I don't want to stay in this body any longer!" This body in which I have taken up residence. I see it. It is short-lived. Of course I am something more. So incomprehensibly more. This body is completely alien to me. I don't even remember which sex I am. Now I am convinced that the body is only a temporary dwelling. That it is not me at all.

Death, my companion, returns. This time I haven't got the strength to struggle with him. I know that he has been with me ever since I was born. Age must take its course. He is a faithful companion. Quite harmless, too. He belongs to the realm of Earth. Where my consciousness is, there is no Death.

° ° °

I am at the end of the road. Here I bring my experiments to a close.

The final experience went beyond all bounds. Psychology has always known that human consciousness may be divided into the conscious ego, and that which is unconscious. But one thing is to think it, to read about it, to concern oneself with it in theory, to catch a glimpse of it behind the door, as I have done. It's quite another matter to experience it in such overwhelming abundance. To experience this tremendous ocean of people and events and other lives that we have inside us, come in contact with. I don't know. But in relation to all this, the conscious ego is so infinitesimal. This remarkable realization that "you are nothing" gives one food for thought. Indeed, humankind is truly a mystery.

Today, we hear about so-called "multiple personalities"—people with several, entirely different 'individuals' inside them, who perform outwardly. In light of all the lives and events we carry with us in the unconscious, the multiple personality phenomenon is quite comprehensible. We all have a number of personalities inside us. With people in whom these personalities perform more actively in their outer lives, in all likelihood, the door to the unconscious is more open. The different inner personalities have an opportunity to slip out and manifest themselves more clearly. But we also see traces of them in ordinary women and men if we take a closer look. Why do so many teenagers want to become actors, play roles?

° ° °

I have knocked at the door of the mystery. I can come no further. This mystery called Life.

Now I understand what the Luminous Being meant when she said, "You know nothing. About the truth of your life." I thought I knew. But it was a lie.

I assume that we human beings will continue to knock. Curiosity has been one of our prime motivations, ever since we took a bite out of the apple. This must be part of the Creation. The Creator must have intended for us to be like this.

I dare say we must allow the mystery to remain. And what difference does it make? The beauty of it is that there are mysteries to delight us every single day. We encounter them everywhere in nature. If we open our eyes and *see*. See the unusual in the ordinary. That a bird is not merely a bird.

° ° °

Every inner journey is a crisis, a study in self-knowledge. And we receive exactly what we need, wherever we find ourselves, the next step along the way. A mirror is held up to us. We see ourselves as we really are. Not the way we think we are. Lies that we have concealed from ourselves are laid bare. It is painful. But once one is through, one is able to forgive oneself so that it is possible to live with oneself.

A deep peace has settled upon me. It is good to be alive. I look out over the meadows, trees and water. A low, red sun colors the warm air pink. What a beautiful planet we have chosen for our temporary residence!

I think: God is in this sun, in these trees, in this water. Not the vindictive God created by man. But a God as unfathomable mystery. Consciousness above all consciousness. The God of love.

"Well-being is something you find in your body," a wise man once said. My body feels good. The pain in my back is gone. I dare say, I choose to remain in this body. For a while.

Here on this earth is where I belong. For the time being. Here I can learn to love, create, understand, help. Here is my responsibility. And I must accept the pain. Understand with Jung: "There is no birth of consciousness without pain." Humans cannot flee from the world of humankind. Love and pain are the world of humans. Our task must be to elevate it.

Anne comes over to me, places her hand on my shoulder. I look up at her. "You know," I say, "I think I have completed my book."

"Do you know who you are now?" she smiles.

"I have asked, at any rate."

"What are you thinking about?" she says.

I must have looked pensive.

"I wonder if the whole thing is a tragedy or a comedy."

"What do you think?"

"I think... that the Divinity must have quite a sense of humor."

"Why?"

"Well, if the whole thing isn't play, then it is meaningless."

"Only play has meaning?"

"From a cosmic perspective... I think... yes."

° ° °

Our hotel room has been burglarized. The police station in Santa Rosa has sent a policewoman to inspect the scene of the crime. I see her while Anne is attending a lecture. I think it is Rupert Sheldrake. We are attending an international congress on "Transpersonal Psychology." The policewoman is long-legged, young, blonde.

She soon discovers that the thief has climbed in through the window. Our money is missing. I discover that my wedding ring is gone.

I took it off when we came to this conference, with 1000 others—psychologists and scientists from many countries. Anne has stopped wearing hers.

The policewoman leaves. I remain in the room. Too late to attend the afternoon session, at any rate.

The ring was two hundred years old. On the outside was engraved a cross, an anchor and a heart—faith, hope and love—on the inside "Anne." I was very fond of that ring.

Now it is gone. I look at my hand. I liked my hand with that ring on it. The first ring I have ever worn.

The afternoon passes. Rupert Sheldrake must have finished. Now it is Marilyn Ferguson, Charles Tart, Stanislav Grof or one of the fifty other lecturers. I remain in the half-darkened room. The energy has left me. The ring meant more than just a ring.

I think—love needs nourishment in order to live. Nourishment from sharing the sorrows and pleasures of everyday life. Speaking one's mind. Sometimes this kind of nourishment is an act of will. Love needs good will. It is a decision.

Anne comes back.

"So this is where you are."

"A cop was here."

"What did he say?"

"It was a she."

"Was she pretty?"

"Yes."

Anne waits. "Well...?"

"Do you know what? My ring is gone."

"Where was it?"

"I'd taken it off... It was with the money."

"You took it off? And now it is gone?" Anne looks at me thoughtfully. "Could this be symbolic?" she says. "What does it tell you?"

We look at each other. I say it: "That the time has come to break up."

She nods.

I continue: "You are moving on. I am moving on. And not in the same direction."

She says, "It's hard when it's said so forthrightly."

We are in different cycles. Anne is on the threshold of a new career, new people in her life, and undoubtedly feels that she cannot be hampered by a marriage. I... well, what do I want? A relationship, I think, in which the relationship itself—making it into a creative spiritual dimension in itself—is what is most important to me.

A relationship is an act of creation. It is created in the same way as a poem or a symphony. The commitment, the patience, the demands for honesty are the same. And also the joy of creating. The creative process is the goal in itself. If one believes that the creation is complete, it is dead.

I take her in my arms. "Let us close the door gently," I say, "not slam it."

I assume this is what we are in process of doing. It has been a year since we went to the lawyer, the divorce which we called off. We needed this year. At the time, we weren't ready yet.

She reads my thoughts, says, "*Now* we can continue as the best of friends."

"Yes," I say. "I feel a kind of consummation."

"Our relationship was necessary," she says. "We needed it as an apprenticeship. To me, it was the chance to proceed. I had reached a deadlock."

I take her hand.

"The fact that I knew you loved me," she continues, "gave me self-confidence."

"Good!" I say.

"Through our relationship I have become a new woman. Previously I did what I thought I ought to do. Now I do what I want to do." She looks at me. "I don't know what I have taught you."

"Understanding," I say. "I dare say that this is what life is all about. The purpose of life, in a way. Arriving at a greater understanding."

"What do you understand?"

"To begin with, in our relationship, I was concerned with what *I* could get out of it." I smile. "I understand that."

She strokes my cheek. "It has been difficult. Four difficult years."

"Yes. I wouldn't have missed a minute of them."

"No," she says. "How could anyone be other than grateful to someone who has loved one so much?"

"That was putting it nicely. Think if that were the keynote of every divorce."

"Yes. If only people could realize that they have been necessary to each other."

There is a pause. Anne stares into space. I say, "You've grown more distant lately."

"I know. It's as if I'm building up distance, in order that parting will be less painful."

"It makes it more painful being together."

"I don't know what is best. I only know that we must be free to go wherever life takes us."

We sit for a while without saying anything.

"I hope they don't melt the ring," I say. "I hope the right person buys it. And that it becomes a symbol of a new experience of love."

"That person is going to wonder: who was Anne?"

"That person won't be the only one," I say. "I wonder what life was like for the one who had the ring before me."

"The name engraved on it was illegible."

"Then the ring had been on the finger for many years."

The room has become dark. Anne lights a candle. We always bring one with us.

"I feel a fellowship," I say, "with these other, nameless ones, before and after me. It would be too commonplace to say that the ring brings happiness. Challenge, growth, joy at times, I presume this is happiness." Anne's eyes are black in the light of the candle. I continue: "And now, without it, I feel an emptiness."

"It will be filled. For both of us."

"Yes."

Automatically, I make the accustomed movement of twisting the ring.

"You have been such a tremendous part of my life," I say.

"I know that."

"Oh God, how I have loved you!"

A wave wells up from somewhere inside me. It clutches my heart. Turns me upside down.

"I don't understand," I say. "Now I thought that at last I understood. Everything."

"What don't you understand?"

"Us... I only feel confused."

Anne gets up, goes over and draws the curtain. I follow her with my eyes.

She turns toward me. "The case is that I have this urge within me."

I know that, but nevertheless... "I've tried so hard," I say, "in my head, to tell myself: It's over. It's O.K. It's best for both of us."

"Yes."

"It's just that... that I still love you."

Anne sits down. She is completely silent.

I look at her for a long time. What's going on inside her? "You once said that I had taught you what love is."

"Perhaps I still have a way to go."

Fragments of thoughts I have thought go through my head. "One day it will wash against a shore in your mind," I say.

"Love?"

"Yes."

"I have been asking myself," she says.

"Love doesn't ask, I think. It just is."

I stand up. I have to shake this off.

"Then let us part forever!" I exclaim. "Cut these ties. I also want to be free!"

There is a pause. Anne studies me. "You believe that I don't love you," she says. "I do."

"Then you must face the consequences of it! Once and for all!"

I sit down opposite her. We sit without saying anything. Staring at each other. I know that I am bound to this woman. I believe she is bound to me.

A smile spreads over our faces.

Anne speaks first. "Only one thing... You mustn't expect too much."

"I expect—everything!"

"Don't be disappointed again!"

"I would rather go all out. And be disappointed."

"Can you stand that?"

"You do, as well."

"Do you think so?" Her voice is tender. "Then we have come a long way."

Where does this jubilation in me come from?

"Actually, it is comical," I say, "that we take ourselves so terribly seriously."

"Comical?"

"Yes, comical," I say. "I feel that this long journey, that I have undertaken, has gone from tragedy, by way of melodrama, to comedy. Of course we must take life seriously, but not so seriously."

"You're right about that, humor is the highest level... Is this the end of the line?"

"There is no end of the line. We mustn't deceive ourselves into believing that. It goes on infinitely."

I hold out my hand to her, with the palm up. She places her hand in mine.

"Would you like to come along," I ask, "on the infinite, humorous journey?"

"If I can keep my freedom."

"I promised to support your growth."

"And I yours."

"Remind me of it, then, in case I forget it!"

"And you remind me!"

"The exciting thing is, we have no idea of where it is going to take us."

I gaze into her brown eyes, the same eyes that looked at me straight across the floor in "The Big Room."

"Remember," I say and smile, "I have come for you."

The curtains flutter in the open door to the balcony. The warm California breeze is welcome.

Other Books Published by MUSE

The Transformative Vision/Reflections on the Nature and History of Human Expression by José Argüelles - art and cultural history treatise tracing split between art and science in western culture; call for uniting these two aspects into wholeness to help in cleaning up the planet.

In Search of the Drum by Ailo Gaup (translated from Norwegian) - novel about Jon's search for one remaining shamanic drum that will help bring back the ancient wisdom of his tribal people, the Sami.